The BHS
Training Manual
for the
PTT

NOTE FOR STUDENTS

If read in conjunction with The BHS Instructors' Manual for Teaching Riding and The BHS Manual of Equitation this manual will provide a sound theoretical foundation and prepare students for their PTT.

The BHS
Training Manual
for the
PTT

The British Horse Society
Registered Charity No. 210504

Islay Auty FBHS

KENILWORTH PRESS

First published in 2005 by
Kenilworth Press Ltd
Addington
Buckingham
MK18 2JR

British Library Cataloguing in Publication Data
A catalogue record for this book is available from the British Library.

ISBN 1-872119-84-0

Layout by Kenilworth Press
Line drawings by Dianne Breeze

Printed in Great Britain by Alden Press, Oxford

Contents

Picture Acknowledgements

All line drawings are by **Dianne Breeze**.

Picture sources
The author and publishers wish to acknowledge the following books as sources for the illustrations:

- **The BHS Manual of Equitation**, Consultant Editor Islay Auty FBHS, published by Kenilworth Press

- **Learn to Ride with the BHS**, by Islay Auty FBHS, published by Kenilworth Press

- **The BHS Instructors' Manual for Teaching Riding**, by Islay Auty FBHS, published by Kenilworth Press

How to Use this Book

The aim of this book is to provide students working towards the Preliminary Teaching Test with detailed guidance on how to prepare thoroughly for the examination.

You will find that the book echoes the structure of the syllabus and follows a clear pattern. The syllabus itself is divided into **elements** under specific headings (e.g. class lesson on the flat, written paper, etc.). For each element you will find information on '**What the examiner is looking for**', followed by advice on '**How to become competent**'.

The syllabus elements marked **C** (compulsory) cover work which will almost certainly be examined or covered in some aspect in the exam. Those marked **S** (supporting) include work which may be examined during the exam and which is considered as supplementary, enhancing the basic standard of knowledge required from you.

It is important to realise that you can never achieve competence purely by reading a book, or indeed any number of books. Books can enhance and assist you in your study, but teaching riding is a very practical subject. It is up to you to ensure that your competence develops from practical experience, through observing lessons given by well-qualified or experienced teachers, and by developing your own practical teaching skills in as many controlled supervised situations as you can.

Ideally this book should be used in conjunction with the following publications: *The BHS Instructors' Manual for Teaching Riding* and *The BHS Manual of Equitation*.

Understanding the PTT Exam

You will by now have had some experience of taking exams yourself, either through Pony Club tests, in taking your BHS Stage 1 and 2, or NVQ assessment and verification, but the PTT is likely to be the first time that you are examined as a teacher.

It is therefore helpful during your training if you have had some genuine experience of riders who are novices or even complete beginners. You can gain this experience in the following ways:

- By observation in a commercial riding school of weekly riders of different ages and abilities.

- By leading novice children or adults in lessons under the supervision of a qualified instructor. This could be done in association with a commercial riding school.

- By helping novice or beginner riders to lead their horses to the school, adjusting stirrups and girths and helping them again at the end of a lesson.

- By watching as many lessons as you can, given by more experienced instructors.

These opportunities allow you to appreciate just how limited the complete beginner's experience might be. It should help you to remember never to assume that a rider knows something already and to ensure that you teach every aspect of a lesson.

Study the syllabus carefully and discuss with your trainer where your weak areas might be, as well as your strengths. Make a plan for developing confidence and competence in the areas where you feel less secure. For example, if you feel nervous standing up and giving a short lecture, make sure that you take every opportunity to practise this by talking to groups of friends, family or informal gatherings so that you develop confidence. Confidence comes with practice and learning to teach takes time and practice.

You must feel confident about:

- Projecting your own voice from the start of the lesson.

- Teach according to what is happening in front of you, not to a stereotyped plan which may not apply to the pupils you have.

- Adhering to clear basic principles such as good basic position, application of the aids and control and understanding of the horse.

- Progressing the lesson in the way you believe is in the best interests of the class or individual, **not** because you think the examiners want to see you do something particular.

Your own presentation is important because it will give you an air of authority and image, which is important for an instructor.

- Make sure that you have a hat, whip and gloves close by so that in extreme cases you could ride a pupil's horse that was behaving badly. If you teach in your hat the chin strap may be undone so that you can speak easily.

- Dress as for previous exams (beige or fawn breeches, boots, shirt and tie and hacking jacket, have top coat or waterproof in case it is either cold or wet).

- Your image should be neat, tidy and professional.

Typical exam turnout – neat, tidy and professional.

The examiner will be looking for competence in teaching correct basic principles. You must be able to:

- Demonstrate self-confidence.

- Show an ability to project your voice both indoors and outside, and maintain an audible voice throughout.

- Control your pupils.

- Progress your pupils to some benefit and improvement.

- Deal with simple situations as they arise (e.g. if a horse is apparently lame, you must comment on it; if a rider appears worried, you must attempt to address the problem).

- You must demonstrate a competence to discuss basic lesson plans for a variety of teaching situations.

If at any stage the examiner feels that you are drifting away from developing your lesson satisfactorily, then he or she may suggest that you take a certain path (e.g. introduce jumping position if you are giving a jump lesson and have spent rather too long on the flat). Always regard this as a help, not an

TYPICAL EXAM TIMETABLE

Maximum 12 Candidates

8.30	All candidates	Assemble and Briefing
9.00	1 & 2	Class Lesson
	3,4,5,6	Written Paper (30 mins)
9.15	7,8,9,10,11,12	Lectures, accident procedure,& business knowledge questions (60 mins)
9.40	3 & 4	Class Lesson
10.20	5 & 6	Class Lesson
11.00	7 & 8	Class Lesson
	9,10,11,12	Written Paper (30 mins)
11.15	1,2,3,4,5,6	Lectures, accident procedure,& business knowledge questions (60 mins)
11.40	9 & 10	Class Lesson
12.20	11 & 12	Class Lesson
	1,2,7,8	Written paper (30 mins)
1.00	LUNCH	
2.00	1,2,3,4,5,6	Lunge novice adult 3/4 candidates OR Lead rein lesson for beginner 2/3 candidates
	7,8,9,10,11,12	Teaching Theory inc. Sports Psychology Child Protection Awareness (60 mins)
3.00	1,2,3,4,5,6	Teaching Theory inc. Sports Psychology Child Protection Awareness (60 mins)
	7,8,9,10,11,12	Lunge novice adult 3/4 candidates OR Lead rein lesson for beginner 2/3 candidates
4.00	EXAM ENDS - Results sent by post	

interference – the examiner is aiming to help you to show your best and is usually more aware of the time limitations of the exam than you are.

On arrival at the exam centre for your Preliminary Teaching Test, you will be briefed by the chief examiner, who will introduce the team of examiners for the day. The day's events will be explained to you and there will be a

TYPICAL EXAM TIMETABLE

Maximum 12 Candidates
The same examiner is used for both Theory sections of the exam in order to avoid duplication of questions.

Time	Candidates	Activity
8.30am	All candidates	Assemble & Briefing
9.00am	1 & 2	Class lesson (40 mins)
9.00am	5,6,7,8,9,10,11,12	Prepare lectures. (15 mins - no examiner)
9.00am	3 & 4	Written Paper (30 mins - Invigilator required)
9.15am	7,8,9,10,11,12	Lectures & All theory (30 mins lectures followed by 60 mins theory)
9.40am	3 & 4	Class lesson (40 mins)
9.40am	1,2,5 & 6	Written Paper (30 mins - invigilator required)
10.20am	5 & 6	Class lesson (40 mins)
10.30am	1,2,3 & 4	Prepare lectures. (15 mins - no examiner)
11.00am	1,2,3,4,5,6	Lectures & ALL theory (30 mins lectures followed by 60 mins theory)
11.00am	7 & 8	Class lesson (40 mins).
11.00am	9 & 10	Written Paper (30 mins - Invigilator required)
11.40am	9 & 10	Class lesson (40 mins)
11.40am	7,8,11 & 12	Written Paper (30 mins - invigilator required)
12.20pm	11 & 12	Class lesson (40 mins)
1.00 - 2.00pm	Lunch	
2.00pm	1 - 12	Lunge & Lead Rein Lessons x 6/8 lunge x 6/x4 Lead Rein (20 mins per lesson)
3.20pm		EXAM ENDS - Examiners confer & send out results.

programme clearly listed for your benefit. (Typical exam day timetables are shown on pages 10 and 11) The chief examiner will give each candidate a piece of paper on which there will be:

- A number.

- A subject for your class lesson (which will either be a lesson on the flat or one involving poles or jumps).

- A subject for your five-minute lecture.

- Whether you are required to give a lead-rein or a lunge lesson in the afternoon.

You need to be aware that an overall 'pass' is dependent on achieving success in a minimum number of Compulsory and Supporting elements – see the specimen results sheet opposite. An 'x' in a box adjacent to an element means that you have been unsuccessful in that element.

The result sheet will be sent to you a few days after taking the exam and, if you have been successful, you will receive a certificate of achievement as well.

Once you have passed your PTT and Stage 3 exam you can start building up your 500 hours' practical teaching experience, which will result in your being awarded the British Horse Society Assistant Instructor's Certificate.

You can begin to 'log' your teaching experience once you have passed Stage 2 and the PTT. The Examinations Office at Stoneleigh will send you a blue log book in which to do this.

Teaching experience can take the form of individual or class lessons, be they Pony Club, Riding Club, riding school or privately. In all instances you should record the lesson in your log book with the name and address of the person(s) you have taught. If you teach a number of hours in one establishment, it is acceptable for the chief instructor to endorse the lessons you have taught under one entry, as long as (if necessary) that person can verify the actual clients whom you taught.

Some of your practical experience can take the form of practical or theory stable management sessions; and you can also accumulate some 'hours' by attending official teaching technique training days run by The British Horse Society. To find out where these courses may be running look in the BHS

PTT

The British Horse Society
Registered Charity No. 210504

BHS PRELIMINARY TEACHING TEST

Result Sheet

Examination Centre: _____ Date: _____

Chief Examiner: _____

Examiner for elements: _____ inclusive _____

Examiner for elements: _____ inclusive _____

Examiner for elements: _____ inclusive _____

_____

Candidate Name & Number

PASSED / FAILED

To be read in conjunction with the assessment criteria detailed in the PTT syllabus.

BHS Preliminary Teaching Test						Unit code number S3PTTE			
Topic	C = Compulsory element S = Supporting element X adjacent to an element number indicates an unattained element								X adjacent to the minimum required shows an Unachieved topic
	Element	Element	Element	Element	Element	Element	Element	Element	Min. Required
Class lesson on the flat	1.1.1 C	1.1.2 C	1.2.1 S	1.2.2 S	1.3.1 C	1.3.2 S	1.4.1 S	1.5.1 C	
Or	1.5.2 C	1.6.1 S	1.7.1 C	1.8.1 S					
Class lesson using ground poles or jumps	2.1.1 C	2.1.2 C	2.2.1 S	2.2.2 S	2.3.1 C	2.3.2 S	2.4.1 S	2.5.1 C	C4 S4
	2.5.2 C	2.6.1 S	2.6.2 S	2.7.1 C	2.8.1 S				
Written Paper	3.1.1 C	3.2.1 C							C2
Lecturette	4.1.1 C	4.2.1 S	4.2.2 C	4.3.1 C	4.4.1 C				C2 S1
Business Knowledge/ Yard Organisation	5.1.1 S	5.1.2 C	5.1.3 S	5.1.4 C	5.1.5 C	5.2.1 S	5.2.2 S	5.3.1 C	C2 S2
	5.4.1 S								
Teaching theory	6.1.1 S	6.2.1 C	6.3.1 S	6.4.1 C	6.5.1 C	6.5.2 C	6.6.1 C	6.6.2 S	C5 S4
	6.6.3 S	6.7.1 C	6.8.1 S	6.9.1 S	6.10.1 C	6.10.2 S	6.11.1 C	6.11.2 C	
Lunge lesson Or	7.1.1 C	7.2.1 C	7.3.1 C	7.4.1 S	7.5.1 S	7.6.1 C			C3 S1
Lead-rein lesson	8.1.1 C	8.2.1 C	8.3.1 C	8.4.1 S	8.5.1 S	8.6.1 C			
Sports psychology	9.1.1 C	9.2.1 C							C1
Duty of Care	10.1.1 C	10.2.1 S	10.2.2 S	10.3.1 C	10.4.1 C				C2 S1

PTT.MarkingSheet(9.7.04)

members' publication *British Horse,* or check out The British Horse Society's website (**www.bhs.org.uk**), or contact your local BHS Development Officer who will have details of any training going on in your region.

If you are a junior instructor in either a BHS Approved Riding School or in a BHS 'Where to Train' centre, and all your teaching practice is done in this environment then, instead of completing 500 hours, you are permitted to complete 350 hours in an Approved centre or 250 hours in a 'Where to Train' centre.

If you are teaching around ten hours per week, then it will take you approximately twelve months to achieve the necessary 500 hours, which should provide a sound practical basis from which to take your teaching ability forward.

The PTT Syllabus

Candidates must show that they have the required qualities, and can apply the basic principles of teaching, e.g. manner, voice, control, etc. and that they have the ability to improve their pupils' horsemanship and horsemastership using a progressive plan. They must know the safety procedures and principles involved in the organisation of a lesson or hack (in the open country or on roads). They will be required to give a class lesson, which may include poles/jumps, a lunge or lead-rein lesson, a lecturette, complete a written paper and join in discussions and answer questions on various topics as detailed in the syllabus.

They must have knowledge of how to proceed should there be an accident or an emergency and have sound knowledge of road safety.

N.B. Candidates may be required to give these lessons in the open and/or in a covered school. Ground poles or small jumps will be incorporated into the class lessons.

Learning Outcomes *The candidate should be able to:*	Element	Assessment criteria *The candidate has achieved this outcome because s/he can:*	Influence
	1.1.1	Use his/her voice with good effect	Compulsory
Class lesson on the flat	1.1.2	Display a manner appropriate to maintaining control and imparting information	Compulsory
Know basic qualities found in a riding instructor	1.2.1	Give a clear introduction	Supporting
	1.2.2	Outline format of lesson	Supporting
	1.3.1	Carry out procedures to maintain the ride's safety	Compulsory
Know methods and procedures used when assessing pupils	1.3.2	Use assessment exercises	Supporting
Give a constructive class lesson to three or four riders of Horse Knowledge and Riding Stage 2 standard.	1.4.1	Use appropriately planned exercises on the flat for improvement	Supporting
	1.5.1	Identify riders' position faults	Compulsory
	1.5.2	Give corrections to improve riders' position faults	Compulsory
	1.6.1	Identify aid application faults	Supporting
	1.6.2	Give corrections for aid application faults	Supporting
	1.7.1	Select suitable school figures	Compulsory
	1.8.1	Give an action plan for future work	Supporting
Or			
	2.1.1	Use his/her voice with good effect	Compulsory
Class lesson using ground poles or jumps	2.1.2	Display a manner appropriate to maintaining control and imparting information	Compulsory
Know basic qualities found in a riding instructor.	2.2.1	Give a clear introduction	Supporting
	2.2.2	Outline format of lesson	Supporting
	2.3.1	Carry out safe positioning of poles/fences and procedures to maintain the ride's safety	Compulsory
Know methods and procedures used when assessing pupils	2.3.2	Use assessment exercises	Supporting
Give a constructive class lesson to three or four riders of Horse Knowledge and Riding Stage 2 standard.	2.4.1	Use appropriately planned pole/jump exercises for improvement	Supporting
	2.5.1	Identify riders' jumping position faults	Compulsory
	2.5.2	Give corrections to riders' jumping position faults	Compulsory
	2.6.1	Identify aid application faults	Supporting
	2.6.2	Give corrections for aid application faults	Supporting
	2.7.1	Select suitable pole/jump distances	Compulsory
	2.8.1	Give an action plan for future work	Supporting
Written paper	3.1.1	Attain the written paper passmark	Compulsory
Select applicable information and record the relevant information.	3.2.1	Show effective legibly written communication	Compulsory
Continued			

Learning Outcomes	Element	Assessment criteria	
The candidate should be able to:		*The candidate has achieved this outcome because s/he can:*	Influence
Lecture Give stable management lecture of up to 5 minutes suitable for HKC Stage 2, S/NVQ Level 2, Riding Club Equitation/Horse Welfare 2 or Pony Club C Test standard candidates.	4.1.1	Deliver the lecture in a manner appropriate to maintaining control and imparting information	Compulsory
	4.2.1	Produce a logically planned lecturette	Supporting
	4.2.2	Relate the lecture content to the brief	Compulsory
	4.3.1	Use props and visual aids if appropriate (e.g. saddle/white board)	Supporting
	4.4.1	Summarise the given topic	Compulsory
Business knowledge/ yard organisation Show knowledge of basic organisation of a commercial establishment.	5.1.1	Outline procedures for receiving visitors	Supporting
	5.1.2	List relevant information required from new clients	Compulsory
	5.1.3	List appropriate information given out to new clients, including assessment procedures	Supporting
	5.1.4	Describe the minimum clothing requirements for new clients	Compulsory
	5.1.5	Give examples of horse/rider allocation, including popular/unpopular horses	Compulsory
	5.2.1	Describe suitable methods of recording bookings and payments	Supporting
	5.2.2	Give examples of client retention schemes (money, hats, children's courses, etc.)	Supporting
	5.3.1	Describe procedures used to ensure new clients are assessed before joining a hack	Compulsory
	5.4.1	Explain client numbers for group lessons and hacks	Supporting
Teaching theory Show a sound knowledge of basic equitation and be able to give clear explanations of lesson subjects and teaching format for the standard indicated of Horse Knowledge and Riding Stage 2. Include the value of different types of lessons. Escorting Hacks. Rider fitness. Lesson structure and content.	6.1.1	Outline the advantages and disadvantages of pupil grading systems	Supporting
	6.2.1	Describe what you would include in briefs for assistants when giving a group lesson to riders on lead reins	Compulsory
	6.3.1	Explain the advantages/disadvantages of private, class, lunge, lead-rein, horse-care lessons and hacks for pupils	Supporting
	6.4.1	Describe an escort's responsibility for the ride with regard to control and safety on highways, open spaces and bridleways	Compulsory
	6.5.1	Give examples of factors which may lead to discomfort or distress in the horse or rider	Compulsory
	6.5.2	Give a description of a child rider experiencing too much physical effort and/or give the possible effects of demanding too much of adult riders	Compulsory
	6.6.1	Outline the general format of a lesson	Compulsory
	6.6.2	Describe a logical progression of lessons from beginner to Stage 2 Riding on the flat and or jumping	Supporting
	6.6.3	Describe a logical progression of lessons from beginner to Stage 2 Horse Care	Supporting
	6.7.1	Give examples of when pupils should hold: the saddle, neckstrap, reins	Compulsory
	6.8.1	Give examples of activities designed to make learning fun for children	Supporting
	6.9.1	Describe how to teach new exercises, e.g. turn on the forehand, leg yielding	Supporting
	6.10.1	Describe how you would explain the jumping position to pupils	Compulsory
	6.10.2	Give examples of how to teach the jumping position	Supporting
	6.11.1	Give examples of the benefits of: ground poles, placing poles, grids and related distances	Compulsory
	6.11.2	Give suitable distances for ground poles, placing poles, grids and related distances	Compulsory

Continued

16

Learning Outcomes The candidate should be able to:	Element	Assessment criteria *The candidate has achieved this outcome because s/he can:*	Influence
Lunge lesson Give a lunge lesson suitable for a beginner or novice rider. Either lesson may be to an adult or child.	7.1.1	Assess and show appropriate handling of the horse/pony for a lunge lesson	Compulsory
	7.2.1	Assess the pupil's basic riding position needs	Compulsory
	7.3.1	Choose work and exercises to bring about improvement in the pupil's confidence, ability and position	Compulsory
	7.4.1	Show a lesson content that is lively and interesting	Supporting
	7.5.1	Develop a rapport with the pupil through good communication	Supporting
	7.6.1	Apply safe procedures throughout	Compulsory
Or			
Lead-rein lesson Give a lead rein lesson suitable for a beginner or novice rider. Either lesson may be to an adult or child.	8.1.1	Assess the pupil's balance, security and position	Compulsory
	8.2.1	Choose tasks and exercises appropriate for bringing about improvement in confidence, ability and position	Compulsory
	8.3.1	Show appreciation of the pupil's age and previous experience	Compulsory
	8.4.1	Develop a rapport with the pupil through good communication	Supporting
	8.5.1	Show a lesson content that is lively and interesting	Supporting
	8.6.1	Apply safe procedures throughout	Compulsory
Sports psychology Have basic understanding of simple sports psychology	9.1.1	Discuss and/or give examples of goal setting	Compulsory
	9.2.1	Discuss and/or give examples of motivating riders	Compulsory
Duty of Care Show a basic understanding and awareness of child protection issues and the way in which these matters may impact on teaching at this level.	10.1.1	Explain the responsibilities imposed by 'duty of care'	Compulsory
	10.2.1	Describe good practice	Supporting
	10.2.2	Describe poor practice	Supporting
	10.3.1	List indications of abuse	Compulsory
	10.4.1	Give appropriate action in response to child abuse	Compulsory

PTT.Syllabus(15.4.03)

If you have recently taken Stage 1, 2 or 3, you will already be familiar with the new formatting of the syllabus, which now also applies to the PTT. For readers coming new to this system, it is clear and easy to follow. The syllabus is broken down into elements which are listed as either Compulsory or Supporting. Within this book the following symbols are used:

        C   =   Compulsory

        S   =   Supporting

You will be examined on each of the main sections of the syllabus and to be successful you must achieve a minimum number of compulsory and supporting elements.

Study the syllabus carefully; the supporting elements are as important as the compulsory ones because they add strength and depth to your level of competence. Do not underestimate the value of the supporting elements – they help to reflect a sound level of competence in the candidate.

IMPORTANT: Candidates are advised to check that they are working from the latest examination syllabus, as examination content and procedure are liable to alteration. Contact the BHS Examinations Office for up-to-date information regarding the syllabus.

Class Lesson on the Flat

The candidate should be able to:

Know basic qualities found in a riding instructor.

Know methods and procedures used when assessing pupils.

Give a constructive class lesson to three or four riders of Horse Knowledge and Riding Stage 2 standard.

ELEMENT

| C | **1.1.1** | Use his/her voice with good effect. |

C **1.1.1** Use his/her voice with good effect.

C **1.1.2** Display a manner appropriate to maintaining control and imparting information.

S **1.2.1** Give a clear introduction.

S **1.2.2** Outline format of lesson.

C **1.3.1** Carry out procedures to maintain the ride's safety.

S **1.3.2** Use assessment exercises.

S **1.4.1** Use appropriately planned exercises on the flat for improvement.

C **1.5.1** Identify riders' position faults.

C **1.5.2** Give corrections to improve riders' position faults.

S **1.6.1** Identify aid application faults.

S **1.6.2** Give corrections for aid application faults.

C **1.7.1** Select suitable school figures.

S **1.8.1** Give an action plan for future work.

What the examiner is looking for

- Your image should be neat with a clean, tidy, professional turnout and from the outset you must indicate confidence in both your voice and body language (Element 1.1.2).

- Your voice must be positive and audible throughout the lesson (Element 1.1.1). Remember to project your voice with clear words which are not hurried. Position the ride near to the examiner when you are talking to your pupils, so that the examiner can hear too.

- It is likely that your riders will be mounted and waiting for you in a line. Introduce yourself and find out your riders' names (Element 1.2.1). Ask your riders if they need help with either their reins or stirrups and suggest they check their girths. Find out if the riders are all mounted on horses they have ridden before (Element 1.3.1).

- Discuss what you have been asked to teach, so that your pupils know the subject matter or aims of the lesson that you will give (Element 1.2.2).

- Demonstrate confidence and ability in your control of the ride as you start to work with them (Element 1.1.2). It does not matter if you choose to work the ride in closed order or in open order so long as you have clearly directed the ride in what

Correct riding position – shoulder, hip and heel aligned.

A typical novice rider position, as yet showing no depth.

Rider faults: rounded shoulders, stiff arms, over-short reins, rounded back.

Rider faults: sitting behind the movement, reins too long, and lower leg forward.

they are to do and you are sure that they both understand and can carry out your instructions.

- Choose work that shows you know how to assess riders and progress the work to a logical plan (Elements 1.3.2, 1.4.1 and 1.7.1).

- Be able to identify where riders have faults and weaknesses and be able to offer assistance for improvement (Elements 1.5.1 and 1.6.1).

- Show confidence in choosing work that will address the riders' faults and help to improve them (Elements 1.5.2 and 1.6.2).

- Choose school figures that help to develop the riders' competence and feel for the horse, from which you can make suitable corrections of position faults or aid application (Element 1.7.1).

- Give some clear ideas for further improvement of the riders by giving them something to be working on in the coming days or weeks after the lesson (Element 1.8.1).

How to become competent

- You will be required to teach a group of three to four riders for between 35 and 40 minutes. The riders should be able to walk, trot and canter and jump small fences. The lesson will take place in a 20m x 40m school which may be indoors or outside.

- Practise remembering names, as it is important to be involved with your riders and forgetting their names does not promote this feeling. If you find it difficult to remember names then take a small notebook or postcard with you to jot down names so that a glance down will remind you (e.g. Sarah – bay horse with martingale; John – brown horse, white brushing boots).

- With any riders for whom you are responsible, remind them to check their girths before you move off and again after five or ten minutes' riding. Be able to adjust stirrups for your riders or advise on level stirrups.

- Safety is ensured by asking them if they have ridden the horse before, have they checked their girths and stirrups?

- An initial assessment of the group is vital (it allows you to decide how the work should progress). This assessment might involve some walk and trot with a change of direction regularly.

- During this assessment, while maybe not yet fully 'teaching' your pupils, nevertheless you should communicate with them, beginning to introduce some strengths and weaknesses in the riders. It is acceptable to work the ride in closed or open order as long as you explain clearly which you are choosing and why.

- With fairly inexperienced riders it is often easier to assess them in closed order rather than have fairly novice riders you have never taught before in open order.

- In the first few minutes learn to assess the basic competence and control of each rider, the basic position, whether they are 'leaders' or 'followers'.

- Choose simple straightforward exercises to start with, going large, 20m circles and changes of rein across the diagonal.

- You must be able to assess each rider's correct basic position and to decide, if there are faults, from where they originate. (E.g. a loose position may be caused by the rider trying to ride with overlong stirrups. Heels drawing up may be caused by the rider gripping with the lower leg and thus drawing the heel up.)

- Watch as many class lessons as you can so that you see riders' positions and faults and what other instructors do to improve them.

- Understand the value of working riders without stirrups (in walk, trot and/or

VARIOUS WAYS TO CHANGE THE REIN

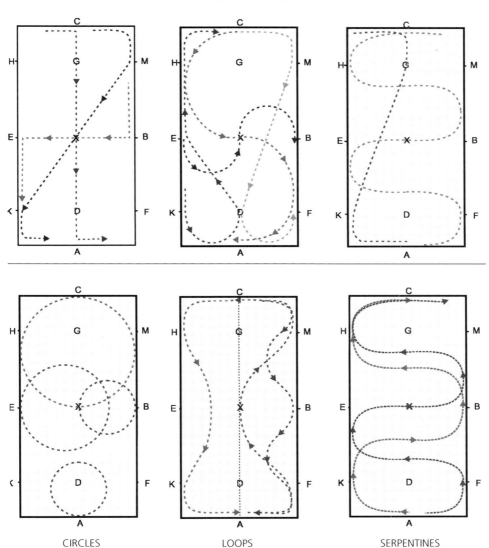

CIRCLES   LOOPS   SERPENTINES

As an instructor, you have a vast number of school figures to choose from when planning exercises. Know them well, and, more importantly, know how to teach them accurately.

canter) to develop the depth and effect of the rider's position.

- Choose work that will not overtire your riders or be beyond their ability, which then may cause a loss of confidence and compromise safety.

- Be prepared to talk to your riders to find out their knowledge.

- It is important that the riders understand the aids for basic exercises (e.g. turns, circles, simple changes of pace and direction).

- It is your responsibility to maintain safety in the lesson at all times and to the best of your ability. You must therefore make clear judgements about what to do and when to do it. This is always dependent on the circumstances 'on that day'.

- Always teach what you see in front of you and what is actually happening. Never teach a lesson that you think the examiner might want to see, or that the rider chooses, despite your being doubtful about the rider's competence.

- Development of the work is essential for maintaining enthusiasm and motivating riders towards further achievement.

Riding a circle. Teach your riders the aids that create this figure: inside rein controlling direction; inside leg on the girth for energy; outside rein controlling the pace and bend; and outside leg controlling the hindquarters, slightly behind the girth.

- Repetition is essential for ensuring that your riders become competent.

- By watching other instructors you will develop a range of exercises, movements and work that will provide the repetition for riders, while also introducing variety to maintain interest.

- As a preliminary teacher **never** assume knowledge. Even if a rider tells you that he or she can canter or jump you must always make your own assessment and progress the work in accordance with **your** judgement.

- **Never** pressurise a rider into attempting to do something that they tell you they cannot or do not want to do.

- **Always** have your full attention on your rider(s). Do not be distracted by anything or anyone who disturbs the lesson.

- Whenever possible, riders should be of similar standard in a lesson. Progress should be directed by the least competent rider in the group.

- Learn to be aware of outside influences which might have a disrupting effect on your class lesson (e.g. horses turned out in a field, galloping about / noisy vehicle outside the school). Awareness can allow you to adapt the lesson content (e.g. come back to walk if working in trot or canter) so that safety is maintained before control is lost.

- Make sure that you understand the basis of the rider being able to ride the horse forward from leg to hand and that the security of the riders' position dictates their ability to apply clear and coordinated aids.

- Practise projecting your voice with confidence throughout the lesson. Clearly expressed words can then be clearly heard and will not be lost into the surface or into the wind if outside.

Class Lesson Using Ground Poles or Jumps

The candidate should be able to:

Know basic qualities found in a riding instructor.

Know methods and procedures used when assessing pupils.

Give a constructive class lesson to three or four riders of Horse Knowledge and Riding Stage 2 standard.

ELEMENT

C	**2.1.1**	Use his/her voice with good effect.
C	**2.1.2**	Display a manner appropriate to maintaining control and imparting information.
S	**2.2.1**	Give a clear introduction.
S	**2.2.2**	Outline format of lesson.
C	**2.3.1**	Carry out safe positioning of poles/fences and procedures to maintain the ride's safety.
S	**2.3.2**	Use assessment exercises.
S	**2.4.1**	Use appropriately planned pole/jump exercises for improvement.
C	**2.5.1**	Identify riders' jumping position faults.
C	**2.5.2**	Give corrections to riders' jumping position faults.
S	**2.6.1**	Identify aid application faults.
S	**2.6.2**	Give corrections for aid application faults.
C	**2.7.1**	Select suitable pole/jump distances.
S	**2.8.1**	Give an action plan for future work.

What the examiner is looking for

- The Elements 2.1.1, 2.1.2, 2.2.1 and 2.2.2. are identical to those in Element 1 for the class lesson on the flat, so it is important that you read carefully the information relating to Elements 1.1.1, 1.1.2, 1.2.1 and 1.2.2.

- With a jumping lesson, the handling of the equipment that you need (poles, jump wings, cups, etc.) must be done with proficiency and competence, through familiarity and awareness of where to place the equipment with regard to maintaining the safety of your ride (Element 2.3.1).

- Ideally, in an exam you will have someone to assist you so that the equipment can be moved into place for you to use without reducing your valuable teaching time.

- You must inform your helper where the poles/jumps are to be placed and you must always check yourself that the jump and any distances have been placed or measured to your satisfaction.

Rider showing a 'light' seat or jumping position.

- Spare equipment should be stacked neatly out of the way of the ride's activity, with special awareness of keeping jump cups tidy and safe.

- You must assess the ride with particular emphasis on the lesson being a jumping lesson (Element 2.3.2). It would therefore be wise to ensure that the riders are riding with stirrups at jumping length before you start. Probably see them in walk, trot and canter and ask them to take 'jumping position' at some stage of this initial work.

- You must be able to recognise when the rider is in a good balance in the jumping position (Element 2.5.1).

- You must also be able to identify the area(s) of fault with the riders' position and be able to suggest help to assist in improvement (Element 2.5.2).

- You must be able to recognise if faults are arising from poor balance or incorrect position, or from poor understanding of the use of correct aids or their application (Element 2.6.1).

- If aid application is the problem, then relevant help must be forthcoming once you have identified the weak area (Element 2.6.2).

- Your choice of work will be directed by your initial assessment and also to some

Working in jumping position over a single pole and several poles.

degree by the 'brief' you are given for your lesson. The 'brief' is a broad-based subject around which you should be structuring your lesson plan. For example, if your brief was to use poles for balance of the rider then you would use only poles. If your lesson were to involve one or two fences with a change of direction, then your plan would be different and include jumps.

- Whatever you choose for your lesson, you must use appropriate distances between your poles and safely constructed jumps according to the ability of your horses and riders (Element 2.7.1).

- You must be able to discuss with the examiner after your lesson what else you might have done given more time and what you would do with the riders if you were to teach them again on another occasion (Element 2.8.1).

How to become competent

- For any lesson of any level you must be confident, and confidence only comes from experience and feeling comfortable and familiar with what you are doing.

- Watch as many jumping lessons as you can, given by more experienced instructors.

- Go to jumping competitions and watch riders competing.

- Become very familiar with how jumps are built, from a simple cross pole to a more demanding double on one or two non-jumping strides, to a vertical fence and an oxer.

- Help more experienced jumping teachers while they teach, but be in the school and help them move fences and put down poles, so that you develop an awareness of how quickly and efficiently you must learn to use the equipment.

- Learn to keep your eyes constantly on your riders; even if you are moving poles with your feet, or adjusting the height of a fence, you must keep watching your riders.

- Never allow a rider to approach a fence if you do not have your eyes on them – and preferably your full attention as well.

- Occasionally, you may still be speaking to a rider who has just completed an exercise but you **must** be looking at the rider who is starting to negotiate the fence or poles.

- In the early stages of your teaching you may need to have only one rider moving around at a time so you do not have too much to concentrate on. As you develop in competence it is acceptable and practical to have the riders working in open order and working over poles using judgement to maintain space from each other.

- Awareness is vital, you must be able to develop a 'feel' for when a horse is getting a little sharp and may start to rush a jump, or when a rider is getting nervous and starting to 'hold back' restricting the forwardness to a jump.

- Watch more senior instructors working with different riders through grids and jumping exercises.

- You must learn basic distances for jumping but ultimately it is how you 'teach' the rider that dictates whether the distance works for that horse or rider or not.

- Take basic distances such as: trotting pole distance at 4ft 6in (1.35m) apart; a placing pole to a small fence taken from trot at approx 9ft (2.7m); a trot approach to a small fence followed by one non-jumping stride to a second fence on 18ft (5.4m); and the same two fences with a canter approach 21ft (6.3m). These distances would be acceptable for a basic jumping lesson with rhythmical reasonable forward paces. However, the teacher must be able to adjust the speed of approach if necessary if a distance is riding too long or short, rather than just identifying the distance as being 'wrong'.

- A basic ability to 'see' whether a distance suits a horse and rider or not is essential at this level. This must be learned through 'feel', awareness and discussion with a more senior instructor who will help you to see what they are seeing and aware of.

- You must teach some basic jumping lessons, use poles regularly and feel familiar with moving poles around and recognising when the poles have been rolled out of place.

- Learn to work in a tidy safe environment and always move spare poles into a tidy stack out of the way of the working ride.

- Always take cups out of stands if they are not needed for a pole.

- Always keep spare cups tucked under the sides of wings or in the spare stack of jumps or in a designated receptacle.

- If in doubt always check a distance if you think it has been moved or is inappropriate, telling a rider to wait before approaching a fence.

- Always choose exercises and fences that are well within the range of ability of your riders.

- Be able to discuss what future work you might do with riders on another occasion. Never rush to build an extra fence or another element to a grid when that might compromise safety. Discuss the option of putting in another fence or part to a grid as a possibility for a future lesson.

Written Paper

The candidate should be able to:

Select applicable information and record the relevant information.

ELEMENT

C   **3.1.1** Attain the written paper passmark.

C   **3.2.1** Show effective legibly written communication.

What the examiner is looking for

- You must be able to put down in writing clear points relating to everyday situations that you might be involved in in a teaching environment.

- The examiner will expect you to be able to write about such topics as:

  - Details required to complete an accident report form correctly.

  - Information required when receiving liveries.

  - Exercise plans.

  - Health and safety guidelines within a yard.

  - Details required for a risk assessment.

  - Information to be included on a 'first-time client' questionnaire.

- You must be able to write the relevant points for the subject given, the facts can be put in note form or under 'bullet points' but the work must be written clearly enough for the examiner to mark it on the day.

- Incorrect spelling will not be penalised but the facts must be clear, concise and comprehensive enough to indicate your knowledge and competence.

How to become competent

- It is important that you have some practical experience of the suggested topics as listed above.

- Make sure that in the teaching establishment in which you train, you consider the systems in place relevant to the given subjects.

- An accident report system should be an integral part of any well-run riding school, as should all the other listed topics.

- An accident report should be completed after any incident which is classified as an unforeseen or unexpected happening, irrespective of whether any injury occurs to human or equine.

- Become familiar with the process of completing full details of the person(s) involved in any incident, information relating to the horse(s), name of person taking the lesson or hack, any other people involved or witness to the situation. The centre and proprietor should be at the top of the accident report. A brief resumé of where the incident took place, including a sketch of any obstacles (e.g. jump or other horses/riders) in the vicinity must be included, as should signatures of anyone who can verify your information in the report. The date and time of the accident is essential and the report should be completed as soon after the incident as possible (while the facts are still entirely fresh in your mind) any treatment (e.g. visit to the doctor or hospital) should be recorded and action taken (e.g. a child taken home, or a parent contacted or informed). It is vital that the person completing the report (preferably the instructor or person taking the hack) signs the report.

- Subjects that could be used as examples for risk assessment are clients collecting their mounts from stables, clients leading horses to the yard and then mounting up in the school or riding to the school.

- Risks could be itemised (e.g. a client getting bitten, kicked, trodden on or not able to manage the tack correctly). A member of staff present to give guidance or assist clients would minimise these risks.

- When leading or mounting, the risks could be getting kicked or bitten (by own horse or another), losing control of the horse while leading or mounting and unsafe mounting. These risks again can be minimised by the presence of a member of staff to assist and prevent any incidents.

- If you were asked to do a risk assessment on giving a group jumping lesson then you should include: field too large; where the jumps are in relation to the gate; how many riders and how competent they are; the ground conditions; using the appropriate horses for the level of the riders.

- Minimising these risks would involve making sure the area to be used was organised in the corner of a field, with perhaps a rope or fence to enclose a very large area. Have the jumps safely positioned, assess riders prior to starting to jump so that the lesson is geared to the level of the riders' ability. Ensure riders have correct footwear, headgear and body protectors if appropriate. The instructor should consider the ground conditions when making judgements about what to jump.

- Hopefully you will have had some experience of your training centre's policy for receiving new liveries. The relevant information here would include full details of the horse (age, size, sex, current feed regime, when last wormed/vaccinated, what work the horse is doing and the reason for him/her coming into the yard at livery. Any peculiarities e.g. an allergy to a specific foodstuff, or difficult to catch if turned out). Additional information about shoeing, veterinary or training issues would also be appropriate. Full information about the owner would also be required, including an emergency contact number. Whether the horse and tack were insured would be useful information to hold. A full list of the equipment that the horse comes with should be made. The horse should be carefully checked for health and soundness on arrival in your yard.

- Health and safety in a yard is a broad subject and, while there will be general guidelines for any stable yard, there will also be specific issues that relate to your own personal circumstances. You must show experience in your ability to itemise the general guidelines (e.g. no smoking, no running about the yard, and sturdy shoes to be worn when handling horses), while also being able to talk specifically with reference to your own situation (e.g. if dealing with a lot of young horses, no horse to be turned out in a field without being led out in a bridle, or, with riding school ponies, no children to be allowed to turn ponies out or bring them in from fields unless supervised by a member of staff).

- Be aware of the Health and Safety at Work Act and how this relates to working environments. Be familiar with a Health and Safety policy and how this might be adjusted to fulfil an appropriate need for your establishment. Consider where the Health and Safety policy is in your yard. Is it written up and displayed somewhere, do you have a copy of it and have you been trained in its application?

- Risk assessments lead on from a health and safety policy and risk assessments are individual to each establishment with some reference to general areas for consideration (e.g. policy for safely turning horses out into fields, policy for safely clipping horses).

- You must understand the principle of assessing a situation or procedure for the risks that procedure may hold and putting in place a course of action that removes, reduces or minimises that risk.

- You may be asked to include information for a first-time client questionnaire. Here you must be aware of the need to record all details appropriate to the client riding at your establishment. This would not only be, for example, height, weight, age, previous riding experience, any disabilities such as diabetes, asthma or epilepsy as well as full name, address, contact numbers and name of parent, partner or friend.

- It is wise to practise writing some of this information down if it is not something you do regularly in your work situation. Learn to put down the relevant points, but leave two or three lines between each part of the work so that when you read it through afterwards, you have room to add extra facts as you think of them, while still keeping the format of the work tidy, presentable and easy for the examiner to read.

- Make sure that you include your name and your exam number on the top of the written paper. It is probably wise to date the paper as well to ensure that it is traceable if necessary.

- The written paper will need to contain enough of the relevant facts appropriate to the subject for you to pass this section.

- Make sure that you are completely familiar with all the health and safety regulations in your own establishment. Offer to assist with the completion of an accident report form. Discuss with your senior instructor or trainer the system for risk assessment within your school. Consider any procedures that have been implemented as a result of a risk assessment.

Lecture

The candidate should be able to:

Give a stable management lecture of up to five minutes suitable for Horse Knowledge and Care Stage 2, S/NVQ Level 2, Riding Club Equitation/Horse Welfare 2 or Pony Club C-Test standard candidates.

ELEMENT

C	**4.1.1**	Deliver the lecture in a manner appropriate to maintaining control and imparting information.
S	**4.2.1**	Produce a logically planned lecture.
C	**4.2.2**	Relate the lecture content to the brief.
S	**4.3.1**	Use props and visual aids if appropriate (e.g. saddle/white board).
C	**4.4.1**	Summarise the given topic.

What the examiner is looking for

- You must be able to give your lecture in a clear controlled voice, showing some variation in tone and volume if necessary (Element 4.1.1).

- Your body language must show confidence and authority (avoid hands in pockets, looking down and talking into the floor) (Element 4.1.1).

- You should try to plan your subject so that you make a brief introduction, then content which includes clear facts and information, followed by a brief summing up and conclusion (Elements 4.2.1 and 4.4.1).

- The brief that the chief examiner will give you at the beginning of the day should help you to plan your lecture. The lecture should relate to that subject or brief (Element 4.2.2).

- If it helps you to use a white board or some 'props' to enhance your lecture subject then these will be available at the exam centre (Element 4.3.1).

How to become competent

- It is important that you feel comfortable when speaking to a small group of people with whom you are not familiar. You must achieve this by practising giving short prepared talks to your friends or co-students, so that you develop competence.

- Gradually try to get some practice in teaching groups of pony club or riding club members on familiar subjects, such as the care of the horse's foot or checking a saddle for safety.

- Practise preparing some of the suggested subjects for the lecture (appendix) so that you have planned the introduction, the subject content and the summary and conclusion.

- It may help you to write out some of the lecture subjects in a small notebook, so that you feel very familiar with the content that you would try to deliver in the five-minute period.

- Think of which subjects might benefit from using a 'prop', for example, 'checking a saddle for safety' would be much better demonstrated by having a saddle to refer to with each of your points of information.

- On the other hand, 'reasons for a daily routine' would not have a 'prop' that would appropriately enhance the subject. However, to put the heading on a white board might be helpful and then one or more headings such as 'What is a daily routine?' 'Why is it necessary?' may enhance the delivery.

- If the lecture is clearly presented and contains accurate facts delivered in an organised way, then it does not matter if you choose not to use any type of prop.

- Make sure that you practise the timing. Five minutes is not very long and it is important not to hurry to finish when the examiner asks you to bring the talk to a close.

- When the examiner asks you to finish the talk, or tells you that you have a minute or two remaining, make sure that you finish the sentence you are starting smoothly and with no change in the pace of your voice. Then state that you have no time left or have been asked to finish your lecture and ask if there are any questions, before thanking your audience and briefly summing up in your conclusion.

- Your summing up should only be a sentence or two to conclude the talk; it should not end up being a brief run through of everything you have already said!

- You will probably give your lecture to the other members of your candidate group and the examiner(s) will sit at the back of the room or aside from the group you are addressing.

- Be confident enough to make eye contact with your audience; preferably stand to give your lecture as this carries more impact and authority than if you sit down.

- You may feel nervous and think your voice sounds shaky but to your audience this is rarely the case.

- If it helps to jot down a few bullet points on a postcard to act as prompters for you, this is fine, as long as you do not end up 'reading' your notes without lifting your head and looking at your audience.

- The list of suggested lecture subjects found in the appendix of this book is not a closed or definitive list. It is possible that another subject may be given to you. If the subject is not on the list then do not panic; consider the subject carefully, and almost certainly you will be able to work out enough to say for the brief period of five minutes.

- Avoid trying to say too much.

- Do give your lecture clearly and with a confident voice with variation in your voice tone.

- Do introduce the subject clearly.

- Do give clear, concise facts about the subject.

- Do use a prop if it helps make your subject clearer and more interesting.

- If you use a white board, write clearly, straight and with correct spelling. If you cannot do this then don't use a board.

- Practise giving these brief lectures frequently if necessary to your friends and family, so that it is easy to do even when you are nervous.

Business Knowledge/Yard Organisation

The candidate should be able to:

Show knowledge of basic organisation of a commercial establishment.

ELEMENT

| S | **5.1.1** Outline procedures for receiving visitors. |

| C | **5.1.2** List relevant information required from new clients. |

| S | **5.1.3** List appropriate information given out to new clients, including assessment procedures. |

| C | **5.1.4** Describe the minimum clothing requirements for new clients. |

| C | **5.1.5** Give examples of horse/rider allocation, including popular/unpopular horses. |

| S | **5.2.1** Describe suitable methods of recording bookings and payments. |

| S | **5.2.2** Give examples of client retention schemes (money, hats, children's courses, etc.). |

| C | **5.3.1** Describe procedures used to ensure new clients are assessed before joining a hack. |

| S | **5.4.1** Explain client numbers for group lessons and hacks. |

What the examiner is looking for

- You should be able to discuss the procedure that your yard adopts for meeting and receiving strangers or visitors to the yard (Element 5.1.1).

- You must be able to discuss information that would be essential to your riding school from a new client (e.g. height, weight, previous riding experience if any) (Element 5.1.2).

- If a new client is starting to ride in your school you should be able to discuss with the examiner what information you would give to the client to help them feel at home when they come for their first riding lesson (Element 5.1.3). You would also be able to discuss your assessment procedure for a new client, to enable you to fit the person into the most appropriate lesson situation.

- This information (Element 5.1.3) would include what clothing they should have as a minimum for their comfort and safety when riding (appropriate footwear, a hat of a current safety standard, appropriate trousers/jodhpurs, no jewellery or flapping clothing) (Element 5.1.4).

- You may be asked to discuss how you allocate horses to your pupils; this would include information about how you encourage riders to ride a range of horses in your school, including those they love and those that they are not so keen to ride (Element 5.1.5).

- You will have questions on methods of booking clients and taking payment for lessons (Element 5.2.1).

- You may be asked about client retention schemes and you should have ideas on these (Element 5.2.2). You should be able to talk about 'pony for the day' days, incentive schemes to encourage riders to book several lessons in advance or reduction schemes on courses or lessons booked in 'bulk'.

- You should be able to discuss procedures for assessing clients prior to taking them for a hack (Element 5.3.1).

- Have some ideas about how many riders should be taken in one riding lesson (Element 5.4.1). This may vary according to the level of competence of the riders, the ability of the instructor, the nature of the work they hope to do (e.g. an advanced lesson taken by an experienced instructor might have six to eight riders, whereas it might be more appropriate to have a nervous novice rider with a less experienced instructor, with only one other more competent rider to act as leading file).

How to become competent

- It is essential that you gain some experience in a commercial riding school, even if you are only able to assist at the weekend, it is still the most valuable way of seeing the clientele of a centre and dealing with the day-to-day issues.

- Consider the booking system initially, see where the school sources its new clients. Does it regularly advertise in the local equestrian press or do riders come through recommendation and word of mouth?

- Are new clients encouraged to come and visit the centre and speak face-to-face with a member of staff? They should be shown around the yard so that they feel familiar with where they will come for their first lesson. They should be shown where the office is, where the loo or rest room is, where the indoor or outdoor arena is and where the horses are.

- There should be a system enabling the clients to look at a daily list and see which horse they have been allocated. In the early days, a client should have a member of staff available to help find the horse and bring it out to the school and mount.

- Be aware that a new rider should be advised on what is safe and appropriate clothing for riding. Do not assume that they will know that a correctly fitting riding hat of a current BSI safety standard is essential. Make sure that you know whether your school hires hats to the client or not, or whether they may borrow one for the first few lessons before being advised to invest in their own.

- Be able to advise on safe footwear, either riding boots, paddock boots or sturdy walking type shoes with a small heel, preferably laced and without a heavy ridged sole. Wellington boots and trainers are not safe, as they may get stuck in a stirrup or slip through respectively.

- Denim jeans can be uncomfortable to ride in, jogging bottoms or a track suit is useful if jodhpurs or riding breeches are not yet purchased.

- The rider should be advised that dangly clothing or jewellery can get caught and may cause injury. Gloves are useful in cold weather as are waterproof coats (not cagoules, which may catch on the saddle).

- Learn to accumulate information systematically from any or all of your clients to include, name, address, contact telephone numbers, age, a person to contact (especially with children) in an emergency. Approximate height, weight, previous experience if any. Any disabilities, e.g. asthma, diabetes.

- Information that the client should receive from you (the centre) would include advice on clothing as listed, procedure on arrival at the school (e.g. book in the office and pay in advance).

- Your aim should be to make your clients feel supported and comfortable about coming to the school, but nevertheless clear about the rules in the centre (e.g. no feeding tit-bits to any horses, only bring horses to the school when instructed to do so by your instructor).

- Some horses are inevitably more popular than others, for lots of different reasons (e.g. more comfortable, less bouncy, easier to ride forward). It is important that you operate a policy for encouraging your clients to understand that they will ride a variety of horses and not always the one they want to ride.

- Encourage your riders to see that their skill develops more as they learn to ride a variety of horses, and that each horse will teach them something a little bit different (e.g. the horse that is easy to canter may not be easy to ride without stirrups or jump).

- Horses/ponies are usually allocated by the chief instructor of the centre or by several of the instructors working together. It is important that a system exists to ensure that horses/ponies work evenly, taking the work load between all the animals. Some may do some individual lessons and class lessons, while some may hack and do lead-rein lessons. A variety of work for all the horses according to their age and ability ensures that the horses stay happy in their work and therefore are genuine to ride. On average and as a very broad guide, fit school horses could do in the region of three hours' work per day over four or five days with perhaps one or two days off per week and one day when the work load is slightly less.

- Bookings may be made by telephone, attending the centre, or perhaps by email. There must be a clear system in any yard so that bookings do not overlap or double book. There may also be a cancellation charge if a booking is not cancelled within twenty-four hours of the time. You may consider whether this system is always enforceable and if not why not (e.g. child is ill at the last minute).

- Payment should usually be taken at the time the lesson is taken. There must be a clear system of recording the payment whether cash or cheque or perhaps by card. Perhaps whoever takes the payment has a code number, or the payment is initialled so that when cashing up at the end of the day, it is easy to trace any problem.

- Many schools will operate incentive schemes to attract clients and encourage them to stay loyal and attend regularly. These may include: pay for ten lessons in advance and receive one free; pay in advance or by weekly amounts for summer courses for children in the school holidays. 'Own a pony for the day' days are always very popular as are 'pony birthday parties' for children. You may be able to pay a small amount per week for a hat and then after a number of weeks you own the hat. High attendance on a weekly basis may also attract prizes or rewards in lessons or kind.

- Assessments, whether for lessons or hacks, are essential in any well-run riding school. Find out what the rider's previous experience is and make sure that you mount the rider well within that experience. Some riders have an inflated opinion of what their ability is. Never take a rider for granted, always find out by systematic appraisal of how they handle the horse, how they manage the tack and how they mount, as well as their riding ability in walk, trot and canter.

- It would be unwise to take a rider out for a hack if their basic ability or confidence was minimal.

- Class numbers will vary according to the ability of the riders, the type of lesson they want, the facilities and the experience of the instructor.

- Class lessons can have between two and eight riders and can give excellent value for money and achieve fun and progress with like-minded people learning from each other and enjoying a common passion and activity.

- Some controlled hacks with several escorts at slow paces may involve bigger numbers. The particular circumstances, rather than a fixed number of riders, will dictate safety. Sixteen riders on a main A-road in Great Britain with one escort would be dangerous; sixteen riders in a tranquil part of Southern Ireland or on the Scottish moors with four escorts on trained trekking horses would be perfectly acceptable. Common sense is the rule, along with adequate assessment.

- Make sure that you know clearly the procedures that are in place in your own training establishment or a riding school with which you are familiar. You can then speak with practical experience about booking procedures, taking payment for lessons, incentive schemes and systems for assessing new clients.

Teaching Theory

The candidate should be able to:

Show a sound knowledge of basic equitation and be able to give clear explanations of lesson subjects and teaching format for the standard indicated of Horse Knowledge and Riding Stage 2.

Include the value of different types of lessons.

Escorting hacks.

Rider fitness.

Lesson structure and content.

ELEMENT

| S | **6.1.1** Outline the advantages and disadvantages of pupil grading systems.

| C | **6.2.1** Describe what you would include in briefs for assistants when giving a group lesson to riders on lead reins.

| S | **6.3.1** Explain the advantages/disadvantages of private, class, lunge, lead-rein, horse-care lessons and hacks for pupils.

| C | **6.4.1** Describe an escort's responsibility for the ride with regard to control and safety on highways, open spaces and bridleways.

| C | **6.5.1** Give examples of factors which may lead to discomfort or distress in the horse or rider.

| C | **6.5.2** Give a description of a child rider experiencing too much physical effort and/or give the possible effects of demanding too much of adult riders.

| C | **6.6.1** Outline the general format of a lesson.

| S | **6.6.2** Describe a logical progression of lessons from beginner to Stage 2 Riding on the flat and jumping.

| S | **6.6.3** | Describe a logical progression of lessons from beginner to Stage 2 Horse Care. |

S **6.6.3** Describe a logical progression of lessons from beginner to Stage 2 Horse Care.

C **6.7.1** Give examples of when pupils should hold: the saddle, neckstrap, reins.

S **6.8.1** Give examples of activities designed to make learning fun for children.

S **6.9.1** Describe how to teach new exercises, e.g. turn on the forehand, leg yielding.

C **6.10.1** Describe how you would explain the jumping position to pupils.

S **6.10.2** Give examples of how to teach the jumping position.

C **6.11.1** Give examples of the benefits of: ground poles, placing poles, grids and related distances.

C **6.11.2** Give suitable distances for ground poles, placing poles, grids and related distances.

What the examiner is looking for

This section is examined with the candidates in a group of up to six. The session takes the form of a discussion between the examiner and the candidates and it is important that you try to contribute on as many different subjects as possible.

- Your practical experience (see how to become competent) must come through in the answers that you give.

- You may be asked about grading riders at different levels of ability (Element 6.1.1). Consider the advantages (e.g. everyone working at the same standard, work chosen by the teacher can suit everyone) and also consider some of the disadvantages (e.g. no one of a higher standard within the ride to demonstrate a new exercise or piece of work for the other riders). Sometimes, in spite of all being the same standard some riders may be more ambitious and hard-working than others.

- You may be asked about leaders for beginner riders in a class lead-rein lesson (Element 6.2.1). You should be able to talk about the age and competence of these helpers and that they would be the responsibility of whoever was teaching the lesson.

- You will be asked in some detail about different types of lesson (Element 6.3.1). Have some ideas about the value of individual lessons as compared with class lessons; there are always disadvantages as well as advantages (e.g. the advantage of one-to-one individual help needs to be weighed against the possible demoralising effects on pupils who have no one to compare themselves with).

- Be clear on the value of a – possibly costly – individual lesson (e.g. for a serious competition rider) versus a group lesson, where there can be camaraderie, motivation to be as good as your friend and a fun social experience.

- Understand the value of beginners starting to learn to ride on a lead rein (or perhaps even the first time on a mechanical horse) or on the lunge.

- Be able to discuss the value of class lessons, individual lessons, group hacks and practical or theory stable management or horse-care sessions.

- Be clear about your responsibility if you were escorting a hack on the roads, open spaces or bridleways (Element 6.4.1). It is important, through the initial assessment and subsequent booking of a hack, that the pupils know exactly how competent they should be (e.g. able to walk, trot and canter independently) before hacking, and that they must take some responsibility for their own control and safety on the ride.

- It is advisable that the escort holds at least Stage 2 Horse Knowledge and Riding because they will then hold a Riding and Road Safety Certificate. If riders were hacking often on the road then this test would be an advisable option to train for and achieve.

- You may be asked about factors in a lesson that might contribute to the horse or rider feeling uncomfortable or anxious (Element 6.5.1). Consider the intensity of the lesson with riders who may only ride once a week. They may not be physically very fit if they do not take any other exercise at all. Even walking the dog, walking to the bus or a weekly swim helps the rider's overall fitness. Hot weather may cause the horses to sweat excessively and therefore become distressed if work is over demanding. The horse may already have done two hours' work during the day and the lesson content should take into consideration the horse and rider's ability to fulfil the work chosen.

- The examiner will expect you to recognise when a child or adult rider is not coping physically or mentally with the work of the lesson (Element 6.5.2).

- You should be able to describe the general format of any lesson (Element 6.6.1). Be clear that any lesson of any duration must have an introduction and a period of warming up both horse and rider; during this time an assessment can be made of both the rider's ability and how appropriate the horse is to the rider. The main content of the lesson will be chosen on the findings of the assessment and the latter part of the lesson should include a clear summary of the work and a conclusion so that the rider(s) go away with confidence and understanding of what to aim for or be able to work for the next time.

- You may be asked to discuss how you would take a rider from beginner level to Stage 2 level progressively and similarly in the Horse Knowledge and Care section of Stage 2 understand how to help someone achieve that level of competence (Elements 6.6.2 and 6.6.3).

- Be prepared to have some opinions about when a rider might need to resort to holding the saddle, a neckstrap or the reins (Element 6.7.1).

- You may be asked to discuss activities that are aimed at giving children fun in lessons (Element 6.8.1) and this should include the use of gymkhana games, teams 'competing' against each other, speed exercises such as dismounting on the near-side, running around and remounting on the off-side.

- You must understand the aids for leg yield and turn on the forehand and be able to describe the movements as if to someone who has limited or no knowledge. Then be able to explain how you would introduce the movements to a novice rider (Element 6.9.1).

- (Elements 6.10.1, 6.10.2, 6.11.1 and 6.11.2) These all cover the development of jumping which will be covered in some detail.

- You must be able to explain clearly jumping position and then be able to recognise when a rider is not in balance in their jumping position.

Jumping position. The angle of the upper body can vary according to whether jumping in show-jumping or cross-country pace, as the rider's balance and ability develop.

- You will be asked about methods to develop the rider's jumping position and these should include practice of rhythm and pace on the flat and include poles as appropriate.

- You must understand and be able to explain basic jump distances (e.g. 9ft/2.7m trotting pole to a jump if the approach is from trot (canter approach is not advisable for inexperienced riders).

- You must be able to discuss the basic grid construction and how to estimate the distances between one jump and another.

- You must remember in all your answers that you must give clear facts, avoid waffling and put across clear ideas that indicate your knowledge and experience.

How to become competent

- Learn as much as you possibly can by watching other instructors and learning from the way they use exercises to improve horses' and riders' specific problems.

- Discuss with the proprietor of your own riding school or a local school what system they use for grading riders. Some schools will try to grade according to ability, some may use age as a guide so that riders of the same peer group are riding together. Some schools may grade lessons according to the size of horse. In this case ponies would work in one ride, horses in another. This is easier when using jumping exercises (especially grids) when distances for ponies may be too short for horses.

- Make sure that you have watched lead-rein lessons and if possible you should have had some practical experience of leading both child and adult riders.

- Lead-rein lessons require a specific competence whereby you must be able to explain the work you are doing as well as lead the horse/pony. Some adults like to be led and in this case be careful that your manner or voice is not patronising.

- Be clear on the brief you would give to an assistant who was leading for you while you are giving a group lesson to beginners. Include how they hold the pony/horse, how they change the rein, how far apart they are from the pony/horse in front, whether they talk to their rider or allow you to do all the communicating.

- Speak to riders about why they have lead-rein or lunge lessons (particularly adults). Find out why riders prefer class lessons or individual lessons. Some riders like the freedom to hack, others far prefer the structure and control of riding in the school.

- Your own experiences as a rider should give you some opinions about the advantages and disadvantages of private, class, lead-rein, lunge, horse-care lessons and hacks.

- If you have the opportunity of escorting some hacks then this can be very good experience. Understand the order in which you might place the riders (e.g. less experienced or nervous closer to you), make sure you have considered the route you are taking and, if necessary, that you have a second escort to assist you. Understand your responsibilities when riding both on the road and on bridleways. Be aware of what you might take with you to ensure support in the case of an emergency (mobile phone, leaving information as to the route you are taking and approximately the time you will be away).

- If your teaching experience covers several months then you should be aware of the variation of seasonal conditions that may cause discomfort or stress in both horse and rider. Cold, wind, wet and heat can all affect the way your rider and/or horse may feel. Overworking horse or rider can also have an adverse affect.

- Be clear on how to discuss lesson plans. Watch other instructors to see how a lesson should develop. All lessons should have a period of warming up, loosening up both horse and rider and preparing them for more serious work. This period also serves to allow you to assess the rider(s) today and give you a foundation for choosing the work for the lesson. The main content of the lesson should then develop and towards the end of a lesson you should avoid starting anything new, which you may not have time to follow through to a pleasing conclusion. The lesson should have a summing up period or conclusion, where work is consolidated and the riders go away with confidence and clear on the work covered.

- Make sure that you are clear on all the work that would be included in a rider's ability up to Stage 2 level and similarly consider the standard of Horse Care expected by Stage 2.

- It may not be long since you were working yourself at that level, so it should be easy for you to remember the progression of your own training to this level and feel confident about delivering a similar format to trainees working towards Stage 2.

- Opinions vary as to how and when novice riders should hold the saddle, reins or a neckstrap when learning to ride. Make sure that you have discussed the options with your own trainer and also watched what other instructors do in different circumstances.

- The author prefers a beginner rider to hold the saddle with the reins until they have learned to rise to the trot consistently. When going from trot to canter the author does not encourage the rider to hold the saddle or a neckstrap as this can give a false security. In jumping, the mane provides a good support to an unbalanced rider rather than a neckstrap which can move or the saddle which tends to put the rider into an incorrect position. Other instructors may favour neckstrap or saddle in different circumstances and gradually you must form your own opinions based on your experience as a teacher.

- Make sure that you have watched children playing gymkhana games and generally having fun with ponies on 'own a pony day' or at pony club camp. Children get much amusement in having the opportunity to plait manes and

Take every opportunity to watch other instructors. Notice how this instructor has positioned herself in relation to the jump, and how she has grouped the waiting horses.

tails, paint hooves and 'dress up' long-suffering ponies in fancy dress.

- You must have a good working knowledge of how to demonstrate and teach jumping position and then to use distances competently in basic jumping grids.

- Be careful that you can 'walk' a distance accurately, avoid talking about 'my strides', 'your' stride should be as near 3ft, or just under 1 metre, as possible so that you can usefully 'walk' distances accurately.

- Be confident about discussing basic distances of trotting poles (4ft 6ins/1.37m), one placing pole to a jump from a trot approach (8–9ft/2.4–2.7m), one non-jumping stride between two small fences from a trot approach (18ft/5.4m).

- Make sure that you can discuss clearly what the movement is and the aids for turn on the forehand and leg yielding.

- The more you have experienced the exercises yourself the easier it is to visualise and help another person to develop the same skill.

- There is no substitute for watching other instructors, learning from what they do and what exercises they use for different situations.

Lunge Lesson

The candidate should be able to:

Give a lunge lesson suitable for a beginner or novice rider.

Either lesson may be to an adult or a child.

C	**7.1.1** Assess and show appropriate handling of the horse/pony for a lunge lesson.
C	**7.2.1** Assess the pupil's basic riding position needs.
C	**7.3.1** Choose work and exercises to bring about improvement in the pupil's confidence, ability and position.
S	**7.4.1** Show a lesson content that is lively and interesting.
S	**7.5.1** Develop a rapport with the pupil through good communication.
C	**7.6.1** Apply safe procedures throughout.

What the examiner is looking for

- The first thing that the examiner will be looking for is a safe and established lungeing technique; without this you will be unable to give a competent lesson (Element 7.1.1).

- Ensure that you are well practised in lungeing and you feel confident in lungeing unknown horses.

- It is essential that you are able to send the horse forward sufficiently in order to give a competent lesson.

- Lunge the horse briefly to make sure that it is going forward and is obedient, lunge it with side-reins attached so that you are sure that it is confident with the side-reins in place.

Lungeing the rider without stirrups to improve position, depth and security.

Stirrup leathers snugly and securely crossed over the withers so that the rider can work comfortably without stirrups.

- Mount the rider (with the side-reins unclipped from the bit) and work the rider first with the reins and stirrups while you make an initial assessment (Element 7.2.1).

- In this assessment, the examiner will want to see you make clear observations about the rider's position, noticing both the strengths and weaknesses.

- As a result of your assessment, choose work to improve the rider. Usually, it is wise to work the rider either without stirrups through some exercises to supple and improve, or without their reins with the same aim (Element 7.3.1). It is not considered wise to work a rider whom you do not know, or a horse that you are unfamiliar with, without reins and stirrups at the same time. There should be plenty of other exercises you can use without needing to take away both reins and stirrups in a first lesson.

- The lesson should be active and interesting (Element 7.4.1). Make sure that you make frequent changes of rein and work in an involved and animated way with your pupil (Element 7.5.1).

- Throughout the whole lesson you must demonstrate safety and awareness (Element 7.6.1).

How to become competent

- I make no apology for repeating that there are no short cuts to competence. You must practise lungeing frequently and with as many different horses as possible.

- Your lungeing technique must be secure and consistent. Make sure that you can manage the rein and whip efficiently on both reins, without getting the rein muddled.

- Make sure that you have lunged a rider as often as possible; if you can, start with a pony (and child) which tends to be easier to manage, and then move to a horse and adult rider.

- Watch more experienced instructors giving lunge lessons and try to have a lesson or two yourself.

- Practise exercises that might be useful to improve riders, feel the effect they have on your position and consider the value they have.

- Gradually develop a range of exercises which work different parts of the body and help the rider's balance and suppleness.

- Learn to lunge a horse briefly and then mount a rider quickly and efficiently so that you do not waste time in this process and can get on with the teaching of your lesson.

- Time is always limited in an exam and the more proficient you can be in getting on with any lesson, the more experience you will demonstrate and the more time you will have to improve your pupil.

- Your safety and awareness is paramount. If in doubt about how a horse might be behaving or reacting then be cautious before taking away reins or stirrups. For example, if a horse is being a bit sharp and unpredictable, knot the rider's reins and make sure that if they do any arm exercises they keep hold of the reins with one hand. If a horse is misbehaving at the other end of the school and your rider is without stirrups, give them back their stirrups as a precautionary measure and say why you are doing that.

- Show an ability to communicate with your pupils; knowing how they feel about the work you are doing, can help in their learning process.

- Your awareness of the correct basic riding position is always of prime importance. Make sure that you can recognise when a rider is sitting correctly or where they are out of balance and need help to adjust their position.

- Watch many riders and their positions and their balance and how this may change according to what they are trying to do with the horse or how the horse is going.

Lead-Rein Lesson

The candidate should be able to:

Give a lead-rein lesson suitable for a beginner or novice rider.

Either lesson may be to an adult or child.

ELEMENT

C **8.1.1** Assess the pupil's balance, security and position.

C **8.2.1** Choose tasks and exercises appropriate for bringing about improvement in confidence, ability and position.

C **8.3.1** Show appreciation of the pupil's age and previous experience.

S **8.4.1** Develop a rapport with the pupil through good communication.

S **8.5.1** Show a lesson content that is lively and interesting.

C **8.6.1** Apply safe procedures throughout.

What the examiner is looking for

- It is essential with any novice or beginner rider that you are able to assess the person's basic balance when they first get onto the horse/pony. Some riders have a greater natural balance, confidence and ability to sit automatically in the optimum position on a horse than others. The naturally balanced confident rider will tend to find more security from the start. You must show an ability to recognise the beginner or novice rider's innate ability (Element 8.1.1).

- Be able to work out if the rider is insecure or unbalanced and know how to make adjustments which will help them adopt a more correct balanced position (Element 8.2.1).

- The exercises you choose must demonstrate that you have recognised where the rider's faults lie and that you have chosen work best suited to improve the security, balance and position (Element 8.2.1).

- You must show an ability to develop a good communication with the rider, being tactful and encouraging in finding out what their previous experience of riding is (Elements 8.3.1 and 8.4.1).

- The age of the rider may be relevant to their level of confidence and understanding and to their attention span and this should be a consideration shown in the way you teach (Element 8.3.1).

- The lesson must demonstrate safe procedure at all time and should show a progression which is interesting and appropriate for the confidence and level of ability of the rider (Elements 8.5.1 and 8.6.1).

How to become competent

- If you can gain some genuine experience of giving lead-rein lessons or assisting in leading while another instructor is teaching, then this will be invaluable to you.

- Watch novice and beginner riders being taught by someone of more experience.

- Watch the inadequacies that the majority of beginners have when their only contact with the horse/pony may be for one hour per week.

- Remember that someone who is able to practise a skill daily or even several times a week will be much more proficient than someone who only has one hour each week to revisit their chosen activity.

- You must be constantly aware of the need to assist and repeat terms and actions which to you may be very familiar but to the novice or beginner rider are still quite alien.

- Be aware that it takes many repetitions of simple tasks to achieve even a basic level of competence, so do not worry that you may appear to be repeating things many times over.

- Try to develop a versatility in repeating the same task or information without confusing your rider. In this way you will keep lessons interesting while ensuring that sufficient repetition does convey competence gradually (e.g. In walk there are many changes of rein that could be used to encourage your rider to concentrate on the aids for turning).

- Make sure that you are competent in leading both ponies (for child riders) and horses (for adults) working evenly on both reins and being able to lead the animal efficiently, especially in trot, while still able to glance at your rider and make simple suggestions.

- You need to be physically fit enough to conduct a twenty- to thirty-minute lesson on foot involving walk and trot and capably communicating with your pupil without getting breathless.

- Be able to lead in a group or individually, keeping a safe distance if you are in a group and using the school sensibly and with awareness of other instructors if you are sharing the school with other lessons going on simultaneously.

Sports Psychology

The candidate should be able to:

Have a basic understanding of simple sports psychology.

ELEMENT

| C | **9.1.1** Discuss and/or give examples of goal setting. |
| C | **9.2.1** Discuss and/or give examples of motivating riders. |

What the examiner is looking for

- You may be asked about goal setting and these questions are likely to come in the theory/discussion part of the examination.

- You should be able to explain why a lesson should have an aim or goal.

- Understand that a pupil learning any subject will be able to prepare and plan their development more easily if they have clear aims or goals set out for them.

- Understand that goals may be short-term, medium-term or long-term (Element 9.1.1).

- Be able to discuss how these goals may be chosen for each rider.

- Consider what a short-term goal might be in a one-hour class lesson of weekly riders (e.g. today we are going to start to learn about diagonals in trot, by the end of the lesson we will aim to have you understanding what diagonals are and how you recognise which one you are riding on).

- Consider and be able to discuss some medium-term and long-term goals (e.g. by the end of the summer holidays we will aim for you being able to jump a small course of fences).

- Be able to discuss how goals might change. (A long-term goal may be for the rider to enter a competition in six months' time.) A long-term goal may have to change if a rider misses riding due to an unexpected illness or progresses more quickly than anticipated when the goal was set. The goal may then be moved forward or back from the original time scale planned.

- Be able to discuss motivation or enthusiasm to progress (Element 9.2.1).

- Understand and be able to talk about what motivates a rider (seeing other members of the peer group progressing, friends or family inspiring the rider, having a clear goal to aim for).

- Motivation is a moveable and fragile state, which can be influenced by good or bad teaching, by a good or bad experience on the horse.

- Riders can be self-motivated or at times need to be motivated by others.

How to become competent

- Consider what goals you have set yourself, or had set for you, during your life but particularly with regard to your riding career.

- Goals must be appropriate or realistic for the rider concerned, they must be achievable and measurable. If they are not any of these things, then often they are unachievable and this in itself can be very demotivating if the goal is unattainable.

- Consider other trainers of riders and consider how they establish goals and what those goals are.

- Watch the outcome of the goal setting and realise that there are times when a goal may have to be adjusted (up or down) to take account of a change in circumstances (e.g. a horse goes lame and then a competition, which was planned, may have to be rescheduled or abandoned).

- Goal setting and motivation have some connection. Recognise that achieving a goal for a rider is very motivating and at that point a new goal should be set to keep the rider's interest and commitment.

- Ask riders (both those you may teach yourself and others) what drives them; find out what stimulates their enthusiasm.

- Also find out what lowers their motivation. It may be things like the winter, cold dark nights, and lack of someone with whom to share their interest.

- Watching top riders on television or video may motivate riders. Talking to other riders and sharing similar experiences may stimulate them.

- Try to watch lessons as often as you can and consider what the short-term goal might be for that lesson, whether it was it clear at the beginning and whether it was achieved.

- Ask other instructors to clarify their short, medium and long-term goals with a group of riders or an individual.

Duty of Care

The candidate should be able to:

Show a basic understanding and awareness of child protection issues and the way in which these matters may impact on teaching at this level.

ELEMENT

C **10.1.1** Explain the responsibilities imposed by 'duty of care'.

S **10.2.1** Describe good practice.

S **10.2.2** Describe poor practice.

C **10.3.1** List indications of abuse.

C **10.4.1** Give appropriate action in response to child abuse.

What the examiner is looking for

- This will be covered in oral questioning in the theory section of the exam. There are likely to be five or six in each discussion group with one examiner.

- You should know that under a duty of care, you as the instructor in charge, should show a responsibility throughout all your time when working with clients for their safety and well-being (Element 10.1.1).

- You will ensure that at all times you work in the best interests of the clients' safety. (You ensure that they have help if needed with the horse they are leading/riding/mounting etc.)

- You never choose work which they would not be capable of carrying out (which would endanger them).

- You understand that good practice is your ability to give a well-planned, well-delivered, clear lesson according to the needs of your pupil(s) whom you will have assessed (Element 10.2.1).

- Good practice follows a safe code of behaviour based on good judgement and awareness of your pupil(s)' needs.

- Poor practice would jeopardise your pupil(s)' safety and well-being (Element 10.2.2).

- Be able to consider what indications there may be of abuse (Element 10.3.1). (E.g. a normally happy and outgoing child may appear for a lesson unusually withdrawn, and may not communicate well with either you or their friends.) The child may lose weight, may be more aggressive or tearful, there may be signs of physical bruising, this may be apparent if in the summer the child is in a short-sleeved shirt or swimming costume.

- Understand that your first responsibility is for the welfare of the child, but you must approach the issue with great sensitivity (Element 10.4.1).

- Always refer in the first instance to the senior member of staff to whom you are responsible.

- Beware of making any accusations without sufficient evidence, and even then be very careful to have a witness with you in the event that such discussion is not constructively received.

How to become competent

- Listen and learn, ask advice from other more senior instructors.

- Fortunately, abuse is a rather rare occurrence.

- Attend a child-awareness course, run by the BHS (see appendix) where you will receive training on how to recognise and deal with children who might be suffering verbal, physical or emotional abuse from an adult.

- Consider the code of practice that exists in the establishment in which you teach.

- Consider how you should follow that code of good practice and conversely what would be considered as poor practice (e.g. good practice ensures that riders are never asked to attempt anything of which they are not capable or of which they feel apprehensive).

- Poor practice could be considered if a beginner rider were to be taken hacking and riding along a main road when their balance and coordination was barely established, and the instructor was chatting to her friend and using a mobile phone, with little or no regard for her pupil. (This scenario would completely lack good judgement and therefore the outcome would be poor practice.)

- Bear in mind that abuse could be considered if a rider were to be pressurised into working harder than their physical fitness allowed (e.g. if a beginner rider were to be expected to work for an entire lesson in trot without stirrups).

Questions and Answers

The British Horse Society Examinations Handbook is an invaluable aid for the prospective examination candidate at any level. The handbook clearly lays out the exact format of each level of exam. How the day will run, approximately how long will be allocated for each section of the exam, and what is required in each section, is clearly explained.

Below are some basic answers to the questions found in the handbook.

- Remember that the questions are as a guide only and, while examiners often ask the questions listed in the book, they are also at liberty to ask similar questions, although phrased slightly differently.

- Be confident to answer any question, as all the questions will be similar and none of them will seek a higher standard of knowledge than those listed.

- Be sure that you have considered all the questions and feel able to add a little more information to each rather than just the minimal answer that is offered. The answer offered is to encourage you to do your own further research and to be able to expand your ideas on all subjects.

Business Knowledge

Q. A new client phones for information and to book a lesson. What information do you need to give? What information do you require from him/her?

A. Information you need to give:

What time lessons run.

How long the lesson is.

How much the lesson costs.

The number of riders in a lesson.

The standard of instructor taking the lesson.

The range of lesson types (lunge, lead-rein, class, private etc.).

The location of the establishment.

Specific information relevant to assessing new riders and introductory lessons to acquaint the new client with the centre.

Information from the client:

Past riding history, if any.

Age if under 18 (and approximately if adult).

Approximate height and weight.

What type of lesson they wish to take.

Q. Discuss ways of running an office regarding bookings, allocation of horses/ponies, payment and how it is recorded.

A. Here it may be appropriate to discuss the specific system that you have used in an establishment where you have worked or trained. E.g. Bookings taken by the secretary or person manning the office; liaison between the person running the office and the instructional staff to ensure that lessons are not overbooked; a senior member of the teaching staff who can mount clients according to their ability and standard of the lesson to make horse/pony allocation; payment made when the client arrives and record made in the day book with a forward booking taken at that time if required, etc.

Q. How do you encourage new clients to become regular clients?

A. Run a welcoming and friendly establishment.

Have horses/ponies that are gentle, pleasant to handle and well-schooled to ride.

Give encouraging lessons which stimulate fun, enthusiasm and learning.

Encourage groups of like-minded people of similar standard to ride together.

Offer incentives to riders to book ahead and arrange lessons in advance with a discount or free lesson for booking a number at a time.

Run any kind of social activity (school outing to Badminton) so that riders feel part of the establishment.

Q. What clothing is essential for beginner riders and how long would it be before you expected correct riding attire?

A. Safe footwear (sturdy shoes with a heel, not a ridged sole and preferably lace-up or zip shoes or boots – not trainers or wellingtons).

Trousers which are comfortable and not too tight-fitting.

No loose clothing, fashion clothing or jewellery.

Preferably gloves and a warm waterproof coat if outdoors and winter.

Correctly fitting riding hat which complies with current BSI standards for safety. (Possible to borrow one from the establishment for two or three taster lessons.)

Gradually clients should be encouraged to own their own riding attire, starting with a hat.

Q. What is your policy when clients arrive unsuitably clothed or wearing jewellery?

A. If the school policy of advising clients before they arrive has been applied then it should not arise. If a client is unsafely dressed then this must be pointed out. It should be pointed out that excessive jewellery (dangling ear rings, bracelets etc.) might be damaged or could be a danger to the rider if it became caught (on this basis it is advisable to remove it). Basic safety – as in hat, shoes and trousers – must be adhered to in the interests of everyone's well-being.

Q. If lending BSI approved hats or body protectors to clients, what advice would you give on how they should fit?

A. Advise that you are not a qualified fitter. Advise that the hat/body protector should fit comfortably and stay in place without the person having to worry about it. Advise that the ultimate responsibility is with them to feel happy with the equipment and, if in doubt, they should provide their own.

Q. A new client wants to go for a hack and not have a lesson. Your policy is to assess everyone in a school or arena before allowing them to hack. How do you handle the situation?

A. Advise that the policy of the school is to assess and that it is for the benefit of the clients to ensure that they are safe to hack. Be polite but do not deviate from your rule, emphasising that your insurance policy requires that you are only able to allow clients to hack if they are deemed of a standard that the school has assessed as capable.

Q. How many riders would you have in a class lesson? Does this depend on their standard? Would you use assistants or helpers and how would you brief them prior to the lesson?

A. A class lesson where much individual attention can be given consisting of four, six or eight riders is practical and increasingly viable economically. More than eight is acceptable, but requires a higher level of expertise on the part of the instructor to manage the bigger number, especially if the riders are of mixed ability or are less experienced.

Helpers can be an asset, particularly with novice riders or children who may need to be led or may need some individual help within the class. The helpers must be briefed to look to the instructor for exact information throughout the lesson, according to the circumstances that arise.

Q. Is it practical to 'grade' riders so that class lessons contain riders of similar standards? Discuss and give the advantages and disadvantages.

A. It is usually an advantage to grade riders for class lessons. This enables riders to progress at a similar rate and is easier for the instructor to manage. Some riders may still progress faster in spite of this policy, but this can provide an inspiration to others to try harder. Mixed ability rides are more difficult to teach to keep everyone challenged at their level and happy with their progress.

Q. Are children's holiday courses a good idea? Discuss.

A. Generally, yes. The children progress by spending a week handling, tacking up, riding and being around the pony/horse for a concentrated time. It is easy to progress to fun activities such as gymkhana games, handy pony competition and fancy dress, things that there would not be time for in usual weekly lessons.

Lesson Structure and Content

Q. What is meant by lesson structure?

A. A lesson that has a structure, has an aim, an introduction to that aim, a period of assessment and working-in when a choice is made on how to move the lesson forward. The lesson then has a period of work to develop the aim following through into a conclusion where the aim of the lesson is consolidated and the riders go away with confidence in what they have covered. During the conclusion there should be a summing up of the lesson and a plan for future lessons or some pointers to take away for the rider to think about or if possible work on for the future.

Q. How would your teaching differ for adults and children?

A. Children have a much shorter attention span.

Children have little inbuilt fear or anxiety about what 'might' happen so tend to be much more trusting of your expertise.

Children may be physically or mentally immature in their ability to control the pony/horse.

Adults tend to want to know more of the 'why' in doing things.

Adults have a greater awareness of 'how far it is to the ground!'

Adults may be physically less agile and supple.

Q. How would you prefer to start beginner riders? Lead rein, lunge, class, etc.

A. Lead rein is often good for small children where the contact is closer with the control of the horse/pony being taken by the leader.

Lunge enables the teacher to have control of the horse but a good view of their pupil and the pupil can take some control of the horse as instructed.

Class lessons enable pupils to learn from each other and to gain confidence from each other.

Class lessons are more economically viable for a riding school.

Lunge lessons are labour intensive (one instructor/one pupil) and intensive on the horse.

Lead-rein lessons can be run with competent leaders under the control of one instructor.

Q. What teaching aids would you like to have available for lessons and lectures?

A. Cones, poles, small jumps (plastic jump blocks) for lessons.

Flip chart, white/black board, video, DVD. Good training books.

Q. How can lessons be kept interesting when the weather is bad and only a school or a manege is available for several months?

A. Involve the riders in pony/horse management sessions, grooming and tacking up prior to a lesson can teach stable-care skills and warm the riders up on a cold day.

Gymkhana games and 'handy' pony/horse exercises and gymnastic pole and jump work can all add to lesson variety.

Q. How can clients who prefer to hack out be encouraged to join lessons when the weather is too bad for hacking – and likely to be for some time due to ground conditions?

A. Run a simple competition within the school for clients in a basic riding (competence) test, basic stable management (perhaps some turn-out and plaiting) and encourage all clients to 'have a go'; this will encourage those who only hack to take some interest in the 'learning' of riding and care skills.

Have some kind of achievement badge, award, star system for clients who take a number of riding or stable management lessons.

Work clients towards the BHS Progressive Riding tests in the establishment.

Q. Exercises have to be taught and carried out well to be of benefit. Give examples.

A. Teaching basic school figures e.g. 20m circle and three-loop serpentine both require that the instructor shows the pupil clearly where the figure goes in the school. Using cones or markers to indicate the four points of a circle, or the points in the arena where the loops will pass, then enables the riders to ride accurately and they can then concentrate on the energy to sustain the pace and the rhythm of the pace.

The instructor may demonstrate himself or use one competent member of the class to show the rest of the class how an exercise should be ridden.

Q. When lungeing a rider what guidelines would you give as to holding – the reins (contact or not) the saddle, the neckstrap?

A. The rider should learn from the very first lesson how to hold the reins (as the reins are an essential part of the rider's aids and coordination so cannot be introduced too early).

At first the rider should learn to hold the reins with a fairly slack contact (leader or lunger will be in control of the horse). If necessary until they have their balance they can rest their hands on the saddle at the same time.

Gradually the rider should be able to hold the reins and let go of the saddle first with one hand, then the other, then with both hands (first in walk only, then in trot).

The neckstrap should be there as a last resort, a 'grab' handle (rather than the horse's mouth).

Q. Explain what you mean by – and how you teach: half halt, turns and circles, impulsion, balance, diagonals, transitions, suppleness, forwardness, self-carriage, outline.

All these need careful study and understanding and the answers given below will only provide the briefest snapshot of a full answer.

A. Half halt is a preparatory aid which warns the horse of a further aid to come (e.g. half halt before riding a canter transition to warn the horse of the impending aid to canter). Teaching a rider about the half halt evolves through the rider's ability to 'prepare to' do something and by this apply their legs into a mildly containing hand which puts the horse's hocks under him and makes him more able to respond to the next aid.

Turns and circles. A turn is a change of direction through a 45-degree or 90-

degree turn, a circle is a curved line sustaining a size of circle from 20m down to 15, 10 and 8m. The aids for a turn and a circle are similar; the aids for a turn are applied and then released after the turn, whereas the aids for a turn are applied for the duration of riding the circle (inside rein gives direction, inside leg maintains energy, outside rein controls the pace and the degree of bend and the outside leg controls the hindquarters with a position a little behind the girth).

Impulsion is contained or stored energy. The rider learns to generate the energy through the legs and a secure position is sustained through the seat and then they can regulate the energy they have created through their rein aids.

Balance is the horse's ability to carry his own weight and that of his rider over his four legs in whatever pace or movement is required of him to enable him to move with maximum ease and efficiency. Learning about balance comes with time and practice and developing feel for the horse underneath you.

Diagonals relate to the rider's position in rising trot relevant to the diagonal movement of the horse's legs. The rider must learn to recognise and ride on both diagonals in order to balance the horse on both reins in trot work. Developing the rider's awareness of diagonals is taught over a period of time and is easiest to start in walk, where the rider has time to watch the horse's shoulders moving forwards and backwards. As the shoulder moves back the foot is on the floor, as the shoulder moves forward, the foot is in the air. Transferring this to trot enables the rider to see which foreleg is on the ground as they sit in the saddle. If the left shoulder is coming back as the rider sits in the rising trot then the rider is sitting on the left diagonal. If the rider sits one extra beat in the trot they automatically change diagonal. This process takes time, patience and practice.

Transitions are changes of pace from a slower to a faster pace or from a faster to a slower pace. They require preparation, clearly applied aids and a developing awareness of timing for the feel of the horse's balance. They are fundamental in the development of rider skill and the correct development of the horse's training.

Suppleness evolves from the horse's correct training and a harmony and balance in the way the rider rides the horse and communicates with him. Suppleness is impeded by a poorly balanced or uncoordinated rider.

Forwardness also evolves from correct training and riding. A horse that is trained to be responsive to the rider's aids and a rider who rides in balance and harmony will produce a situation where the horse is willing to go forward because it is easy for him to do so.

Self-carriage evolves from the horse's ability to carry himself correctly and in balance and with forwardness and suppleness.

Outline relates to the shape of the horse from his croup to his poll. It should be a rounded profile of a convex nature. The hind legs step under the horse, his back is rounded and forming a supple bridge between the activity of the hind legs, the carriage of the neck up from the shoulder and a submissive relaxed contact of the mouth through the elasticity of the poll and the jaw.

Q. How do you explain and teach the turn on the forehand, leg yield?

A. Turn on the forehand is a movement where the horse moves his hind legs around his forelegs completing a 180-degree turn in his own length. His inside hind leg steps away from the rider's inside leg and the horse moves his quarters away from the direction in which he is bent. The aids for turn on the forehand are the inside leg a little behind the girth to move the quarters over, a slight flexion created by the inside rein, the outside rein controls the degree of bend and the outside leg behind the girth controls the speed with which the quarters move over. In turn on the forehand, the movement is ridden from halt, in turn about the forehand the movement is made from walk and the horse maintains the walk rhythm throughout the turn.

Leg yield is a movement where the horse is straight with a hint of flexion away from the direction in which he will be asked to move. The inside hind leg steps under the horse's centre of gravity taking a forward and sideways step to move him from one line to another or along a straight line while keeping his body straight. Leg yield is a suppling exercise and a developing exercise towards lateral work requiring some collection (e.g. shoulder in).

Leg yield can be ridden in walk or trot, the inside rein asks for a hint of flexion away from the direction of movement, the inside leg asks for more energy on the girth, the outside rein does not allow the pace to increase and controls the straightness, the extra energy then takes the horse forwards and sideways, the rider's outside leg behind the girth controls the quarters, preventing them from swinging out.

Q. What do you mean by jumping position or balanced seat when jumping? How do you develop it when teaching?

A. Adopting jumping position teaches riders a position which will help them to be in balance when the horse goes through the three phases of a jump (approach, in the air, landing). The rider adapts his or her position to be able to stay in harmony with the horse as the horse changes his balance through these phases.

The rider adopts a slightly shorter stirrup length (one or two holes) and is then able to close the angles in the joints between foot and lower leg, lower leg and thigh and thigh and upper body. In this more closed position and taking the shoulders forward with a slightly shorter rein, the rider's seat moves back in the saddle and the rider covers a broader more flexible base position in the saddle, the seat is lighter and more weight is taken into the lower leg and heel which is deep and flexible. The rider is in a secure position to move in balance with the horse as he jumps.

The rider should work in jumping position in walk, trot and canter and over poles to establish confidence and security in this position before starting to jump.

Q. What are the advantages of using a grid?

(a) For horses

A. It develops the horse's confidence and athleticism in jumping. It can develop his suppleness in dealing with different distances.

(b) For riders

A. It develops the rider's confidence and ability while not having to worry about the distance between fences. It can bring the rider into exactly the right position for the jumps.

Q. Give examples of distances for ground poles and various ways of using them to the benefit of horse and rider.

A. Ground poles would usually be set at 4ft 6in (1.35m); these would be appropriate for trotting. Poles can be set singly or in groups of three or more to improve the rider's balance and accuracy to ride to the centre. The horse is improved in his early training in work over poles to develop, rhythm, balance and confidence.

Canter poles can also be used for more experienced horses and riders (set between 9ft/2.7m and 12ft/3.6m).

(a) A placing pole to a jump:

With a trot approach the pole would be at between 8ft (2.4m) and 9ft (2.7m).

With a canter approach the distance would be at least 9ft (2.7m). This would be for riders and horses with more experience – it would be less appropriate for novice riders.

(b) For a bounce:

A bounce from trot would be 9–10 ft (2.7–3m).

From canter the bounce would be 10–12ft (3–3.6m).

(c) For a one non-jumping stride combination:

With a trot approach the distance would be about 18ft (5.4m).

With a canter approach the distance would be between 21ft (6.3m) and 24ft (7.2m).

(d) For a two non-jumping stride combination:

With a trot approach the distance would be about 28ft (8.4m).

With a canter approach the distance would be between 30ft (9m) and 33ft (9.9m).

Q. Explain what is meant by a related distance and how would you set it up when teaching. Give examples of distances you would use for three and four strides.

A. A related distance is two jumps, placed in such a way that when jumped one after the other there is a set number of strides in canter between the two jumps.

A three-stride related distance would be between 42ft (12.6m) and 48ft (14.4m).

A four-stride related distance would be between 51ft (15.3m) and 57ft (17.1m).

When teaching, develop the rider's feel for a good rhythm in canter and then start with two poles on the ground and help the rider to be able to feel or count the number of strides between poles. Gradually introduce jumps, keeping the first fence smaller while building up the second fence so that the rider finds it easy to jump in to the related distance with confidence and then build their ability to ride the related strides in a good flowing rhythm.

Q. Moving show jumps can be done with efficiency. Explain how you would carry wings and poles and how four or five fences can be erected quickly for a lesson, using one helper.

A. Keep all cups in a bucket so that they are safe and can be easily carried about and not lost on the floor.

Move heavy wings between two of you. Ideally, use light plastic equipment that is easily moved by one person.

Place poles at the site of where you want the jump and let your helper then bring the wings or blocks.

Choose a simple plan that keeps all the jumps in one area so that moving fences a long way is not time consuming.

If building a grid or combination, place it nearest the jump store, with the plain single jump furthest away.

Q. Is it important for once-a-week riders to have the same instructor each time?

A. The advantages would be that the riders would have confidence in the instructor with whom they are familiar. There is likely to be better continuity if the instructor knows the pupils and can relate to their weekly progress. The pupils are more likely to confide their hopes and fears to someone they know well.

The advantages of having a different instructor would be that a fresh eye can bring a new input or appraisal of the riders.

Q. Do you keep records of progress of riders? Are tests for clients appropriate?

A. It is wise to keep some records of progress for riders because then it is easier to follow through with progressive work especially if different instructors are taking the lessons.

Tests for riders can provide a challenge and incentive to progress for riders. It can give them a bench mark of where they are in their riding compared to e.g. a year ago.

Q. How important is it to be aware of basic faults such as poor mounting and incorrect altering of stirrups, that creep in, despite initial correct teaching? Give other examples.

A. It is vital that a correct procedure is maintained and adhered to in all basic management and riding of the horse or eventually a casual fault will cause an accident.

Other examples: taking a coat off when mounted without either having someone hold the horse or being sure that you keep hold of the reins; lining up too close to other horses and allowing them to touch noses casually or swing their quarters towards each other; crowding horses together when leaving the arena (mounted or unmounted)

Q. You are planning an 'own a pony week'. What will you include and how will you ensure safety in the various tasks and riding activities?

A. One child per pony, each child to be monitored and supported by one instructor either directly if less competent or through a more competent member of the group who has experience of the type of day.

Include catching ponies (controlled and organised) grooming, tacking up, riding, untacking, cleaning tack, care of ponies after work. Some theory of pony care, some fun activity, mounted or unmounted, games or treasure hunt.

At all times the children must be supervised and the activities must be structured to ensure safety and organised fun.

Q. What are the Progressive Riding Tests? Can they benefit the riding school as well as clients?

A. Progressive Riding Tests are tests set by the BHS for adults and juniors (Junior Achiever Tests) to give them a gauge of their riding and stable management ability.

There are six tests for adults and five for juniors and these can be split into riding and stable management.

They can benefit the riding school by giving the school the chance to run courses and training aimed towards achieving the tests.

Q. In a riding school where hacking includes some road work, would you encourage and train clients for the BHS Riding and Road Safety Test? What is involved?

A. The Riding and Road Safety Test is a useful addition to the training and knowledge of any rider who will ride on the public highway.

The test involves a comprehensive multiple-choice question paper on all aspects of road safety as delivered by the Highway Code, but with specific reference to horse riding. (All the relevant information can be found in The British Horse Society's booklet, *Riding and Roadcraft,* published by Kenilworth Press.) There is also a ridden section on a simulated road, involving tests and hazards, and a further section which is examined on a route set on a public highway.

Q. When a client asks you a question that you cannot answer, what do you do?

A. Ask a senior member of the establishment or your own instructor, or tell the person that you don't know the answer but will find out and come back to them on it.

Sports Psychology

Sample questions that should be discussed in the theory section.

Q. Discuss some qualities of a good instructor/coach.

A. Patience

Good knowledge and ability to put that across

Stamina

Good clear voice

Sense of humour

Enthusiasm

Confidence

Authority

Awareness

Q. Why is feedback an important part of teaching?

A. Your pupils learn from the feedback that you give them.

They should be able to build on positive feedback.

It should give them a clear picture of where their strengths and weaknesses are and how to address them.

It allows for two-way communication between you and your pupil.

Q. What do you understand by the term 'motivation'?

A. Motivation is the 'drive' or incentive to want to do better.

Q. Discuss some ways you could motivate: (a) children, (b) adults, during a riding lesson.

A. Giving them a challenge to be better than each other often motivates children.

Giving them a specific aim, which they can all try to achieve, often motivates children (e.g. Who can get closest to the cone in the corner? Who can touch the cone from their pony?).

Adults may be motivated by a more individual aim (e.g. today we are aiming to canter for the first time).

Seeing someone else achieve the goal they are aiming for may motivate adults.

Q. How would you motivate riders who were not keen to ride?

A. Find out why they are not keen to ride. It may not be sensible to try to encourage them to ride if they really do not want to.

Riding is a sport that needs a degree of self-motivation.

Handling the horse and feeling more confident around him before riding him may encourage them.

It can help if they have ridden a mechanical horse, when they need have no fear of not being in control.

Q. What teaching methods could you adopt to motivate a class of teenage riders who have had to ride in the indoor school for several weeks due to bad weather?

A. Ask each rider to choose an exercise to explain to the rest of the class, and then the class ride it.

Make a mini competition on the best rider position, making them give themselves a mark out of ten (one being low and ten being high).

Do the same without stirrups and encourage them to improve on their own mark.

Do similar exercises but ask them to mark each other.

Q. What do you understand by 'goal setting' when teaching riders?

A. Goal setting is setting aims for riders which are achievable either in the short term, medium or long term. The goal must be measurable and realistic to the specific pupil.

A short-term goal might be to learn about diagonals in trot this week, a medium-term goal may be to be able to recognise and change diagonal efficiently and a long-term goal may be to be able to feel which diagonal you are on on every horse you ride.

Q. Discuss the types of goal you could set for different riders (e.g. individual lessons in dressage or jumping, lead-rein lessons, class lessons, lunge lessons and stable management lessons).

A. The answer to this question could fill a small book in its own right. However, to help you answer this constructively in the exam, we will consider some options.

With all lessons the following criteria will help you to set the appropriate goals:

In a private lesson, consider the age and ability of the rider, how often they ride – so how fit they might be.

Ask them what they would like to do (in case they have a burning desire about something)

Consider the length of time you have to teach.

Consider the facilities you have. The goal for a novice child in a safe indoor school will be very different to the goal for that same child outside in a large field.

Consider the weather conditions. A lesson in walk on a hot day may be appropriate, whereas on a cold frosty day it would not.

Agree the goal with the rider. If the rider does not want to canter, that should not be your goal!

In a class lesson, there are other considerations such as whether all riders are of the same or similar ability, and, if you are likely to choose a jumping goal, whether all riders are mounted on horses/ponies that jump.

Lead-rein lessons are generally easier to set clear goals for, because you, as the leader, have total control over the pace of the horse/pony, which allows you to limit any problems that might arise.

Similarly, lunge lessons would usually be directed at some form of rider position improvement.

Stable-management lessons should be directed towards something that interests the pupil and helps them to be a more independent rider.

Listed below are one or two typical goals for each type of lesson.

Private dressage lesson. Improve awareness of rhythm in all three paces. Improve the basic transitions from one pace to another.

Private jumping lesson. Improve basic position using several fences in a simple grid. Improve the rider's ability to canter into a jump.

Lead-rein lesson. Improve the rider's confidence in going from rising trot to sitting to make a downward transition. Basic work without stirrups.

Class lesson. Improve the riding of turns and circles. Improve the knowledge of methods of changing the rein.

Lunge lesson. Improve the feel for the horse by identifying when the hind legs touch the ground. Improve the use of diagonals in trot.

Stable management lessons. Learning how to put on and fit tack.

Q. Consider each type of lesson and the type of goals you might set for an experienced rider and a more novice rider in the short, medium and long-term situation.

A. The potential answers to this question are diverse and variable, and may be influenced by such things as the weather conditions, the confidence of the rider on 'that day', the frequency with which they ride, and other factors. The things to remember are that while planning and 'goal setting' are very important in any lesson, it is also vital that you teach 'what you see on the day' and do not stick rigidly to a plan or goal if that becomes unachievable due to an unforeseen reason.

- As a guide for an experienced rider in a class lesson:

   A **short-term goal** might be to work on the ability to slightly shorten and lengthen the horse's stride in trot, while working for a short period without stirrups to improve the rider's depth of position.

   A **medium-term goal** might be to work on the ability to feel how some horses find it easier than others to shorten and lengthen, and to develop the range in walk and canter as well.

   A **long-term goal** might be to ride one specific horse to develop the range in all his paces, while linking the work to the development of lateral movements, which enhances the work further.

■ For an experienced rider in an individual lesson:

A **short-term goal** may be to understand the aids for turn on the forehand and to begin to be able to ride this movement.

A **medium**-term goal may be to begin to rider leg-yield.

A **long-term goal** may be to have a greater understanding and feel for these movements and how they relate to the training of the horse and the feel for improving the paces.

■ Choice of goals for novice riders would be much more aimed at consolidating the basic learning of things like:

Basic correct position, balance and security.

Basic understanding of the aids, how to apply them and how to develop coordination.

Basic ability to ride transitions (simple transitions between each pace).

Ability to ride simple turns and circles and to understand the basic principles of rhythm, suppleness, speed of the pace, contact between hand and leg, forwardness and balance.

Remember that for novice and experienced riders there are a range of experiences which can be included to develop their versatility and enjoyment as riders – for example, working in the school, in the fields, out hacking in the countryside, polework, jumping, independent riding (alone and in company). All these experiences could be built into any goal-setting programme.

Q. Imagine you are teaching a keen adult rider who has fallen off while jumping in a previous lesson and has lost their nerve. How would you proceed with your lesson/s to increase the rider's confidence?

A. Find out how they feel about the fall (whether they accept it was 'one of those things'/an occupational hazard, or are very negative about the circumstances of the fall).

Consider mounting them on a different horse on which they feel happy.

Go back to basic work in jumping position and over poles without any thought of jumping.

Wait until the rider actually wants to jump again before introducing a fence.

Work them in a group where other riders are addressing similar issues, so that the rider does not feel isolated in their own experience.

Q. If you are teaching a beginner rider who is not making much progress, what could you suggest to help to improve them?

A. ■ Find out how they feel about their progress; it may not bother them that they are not making faster progress and so they are not trying particularly hard.

■ Try to put them in a group where there are other riders of a similar standard so that may help to motivate them to progress as the others do.

■ Perhaps change the instructor or the horse they ride.

■ Perhaps suggest a lunge lesson or private lesson.

Q. What do you understand by the terms 'positive thinking' and 'negative thinking'?

A. People who think positively tend to see the bright side of things; they tend to be optimistic in their thinking and this can often affect their progress. They believe they are good and will tend to do better than negative thinkers, who are inclined to put themselves down and be pessimistic about their progress.

Q. How can positive thinking while (a) teaching and (b) riding affect your performance? Conversely, how can negative thinking affect a rider's and teacher's performance?

A. Consider this carefully and study some literature on sports psychology in the realm of positive/negative thinking. Consider your own attitude as both a rider and when teaching or being taught.

Q. How could you help the rider who has to ride a horse that no one else wants to?

A. Have a policy in the school that everyone rides every horse (according to their ability).

Encourage riders to see it is a positive advantage to develop their experience when riding something that is not liked.

Tell the rider that next week they can ride a horse of their choice.

Q. Can you give some reasons that may negatively affect a rider's performance?

A. Tiredness, illness.

Emotional problems (e.g. row with parent or boy/girlfriend).

Other worries (e.g. exams at school/college, money worries).

Fear of a past experience being repeated.

Q. Why do you think it is important to review a rider's performance at regular intervals?

A. To consider progress and make sure that the rider is progressing at an acceptable rate for them, taking all circumstances into consideration (e.g. how often they ride).

To ensure that the rider is happy with the agreed goals.

To reconsider the goals if some have been achieved and more need to be set.

Q. Clients like to feel valued. Why is this important and how can you ensure they do?

A. Everyone likes to feel valued, it is human nature.

Treat them as an individual (not as a number).

Know their name and speak to them personally whenever you can even if they are not one of your particular clients.

Involve them personally in decisions which affect them (goals, worries, progress).

Q. How can you encourage your clients to keep returning for lessons? What mechanism does the BHS provide to encourage riders to return for lessons?

A. Treat them as individuals.

Be interested in their progress.

Work out a personal plan for their development and needs.

Run classes and training days that appeal to what they want.

Have a club or loan horse system in your school which they can feel a part of.

The BHS runs the Progressive Riding Tests which your school can utilise in many ways to stimulate learning, enthusiasm for lessons and training.

A BHS approved establishment should offer a well-run centre in which a rider can develop their passion for their sport of riding.

Child Protection Awareness and Duty of Care

Q. What is meant by the term 'child protection' or 'duty of care'?

A. It is the adult's responsibility when in charge of children, to provide a safe environment for them in whatever activity they are involved.

The adult has a duty to provide as safe a situation as is possible for the welfare and well-being of any child.

Q. What age group is 'legally' classified as a 'child'?

A. Individuals up to the age of eighteen.

Q. Why is it important for riding instructors and coaches to have awareness of child protection issues?

A. Riding is a very physical sport and there are instances when a riding instructor may make contact with a child (e.g. legging up the rider, going to a rider who has fallen off and is distressed).

The position of the instructor in relation to helping a child must never be in question.

The relationship between child and teacher must always be of unquestionable integrity.

Q. What do you understand by 'good practice'? Give some examples of good practice when working with children.

A. Good practice is carrying forward training that is within the capability of the pupil(s) following a clear pathway of progress with clear explanation of work and much opportunity for the pupil to feed back on satisfactory progress.

Good practice with children would include clear but short explanation of work without overloading or confusing the child with information.

Short sessions of work so that the child is not bored or over-tired by the lesson.

Opportunity for two-way communication with the child to monitor progress and feedback.

Q. What sort of things should be avoided as poor practice?

A. Overwork so that the child is tired or disillusioned.

Over-criticism so that the child feels inadequate and disappointed.

Q. What special considerations or care must be taken when teaching children as opposed to adults?

A. Children may not be brave enough to tell you that they are cold, wet or tired.

Children may not be brave enough to tell you that they are afraid to do something or that they do not understand.

Q. Do you think it is a good idea to allow parents to become involved in their children's lessons?

A. It can be helpful if it is well controlled and the parents do not interfere (e.g. small child being led by parent although the instructor controls the lesson).

It can be detrimental if the parent takes over the lesson or the parent is saying one thing and the instructor another.

Q. What sort of problems could be caused by parents who are over-anxious about their child's safety?

A. They make the child more insecure and doubting of their own ability.

They cause disruption for other members of the class.

They affect the attitude of other parents.

Q. How would you deal with parents who are too pushy or over ambitious?

A. Firmly! Talk to them privately about the standards that the establishment sets and explain that you as the professional instructor rely on them to trust your ability and leave you to make the choices about what their child does or does not do in a lesson.

Q. What sort of things might cause you to have concerns about the welfare of a child in your ride?

A. A change in behaviour from normal (child normally outgoing becomes withdrawn or tearful).

Inconsistent behaviour or attendance from a normally consistent child.

Signs of physical abuse such as unexplained bruising on arms or face.

Q. What would you do/whom would you contact if you had concerns about the welfare of a child in your ride?

A. You must be very careful in your approach.

First you should discuss the situation with the parent or guardian of the child.

You might speak to a close friend (adult).

You might consider talking to a member of the staff at the school that the child attends.

Q. What would you do if one of the children in your ride or on the yard was being bullied or verbally abused by the other children?

A. If you see it actually happening then you must deal with the culprit and in doing so you must involve the parents of that child and if necessary ban the child from attending lessons in future until the behaviour is guaranteed to change.

If you only suspect it is happening, then you must try to get the confidence of the child being bullied or a friend who will give you the necessary evidence to tackle the issue.

You cannot act on hearsay and in every situation must deal very carefully with the circumstances.

Q. Where can you get information and advice on teaching people with disabilities?

A. Through the Riding for the Disabled Association. There is a national office and then most regions have a local group who would be able to offer local knowledge and assistance.

Further Reading

The following books and booklets can all be obtained from the BHS Bookshop.

The BHS Complete Manual of Stable Management

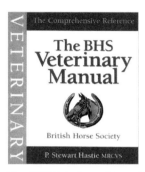

The BHS Veterinary Manual

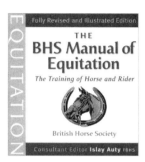

The BHS Manual of Equitation

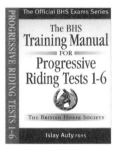

The BHS Training Manual for Progressive Riding Tests 1-6

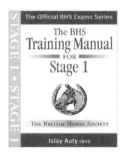

The BHS Training Manual for Stage 1

The BHS Training Manual for Stage 2

The BHS Training Manual for Stage 3

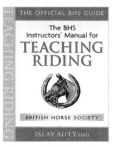

The BHS Instructors' Manual for Teaching Riding

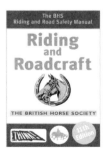

The BHS Riding and Road Safety Manual – Riding and Roadcraft

**Guide to BHS
Examinations**

**Examinations
Handbook**

**BHS Guide to Careers
with Horses**

Duty of Care

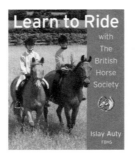

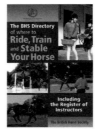

**Learn to Ride with
The British Horse
Society**

**The BHS Directory of
Where to Ride, Train
and Stable your
Horse**

Useful Addresses

The British Horse Society
Stoneleigh Deer Park
Kenilworth
Warwickshire
CV8 2XZ
tel: 08701 202244 or 01926 707700
fax: 01926 707800
website: www.bhs.org.uk
email: enquiry@bhs.org.uk

BHS Bookshop
(address as left)
tel: 08701 201918
    01926 707762
website: www.britishhorse.com

BHS Standards Directorate

BHS Examinations Department
(address as above)
tel: 01926 707784
fax: 01926 707800
email: exams@bhs.org.uk

BHS Training Department
(address as above)
tel: 01926 707820
    01926 707799
email: training@bhs.org.uk

BHS Riding Schools/Approvals
    Department
(address as above)
tel: 01926 707795
fax: 01926 707796
email: Riding.Schools@bhs.org.uk

BHS Competitions Department
(address as above)
tel: 01926 707831
fax: 01926 707796
email: competitions@bhs.org.uk

The BHS Examination System

Outline of progression route through BHS examinations

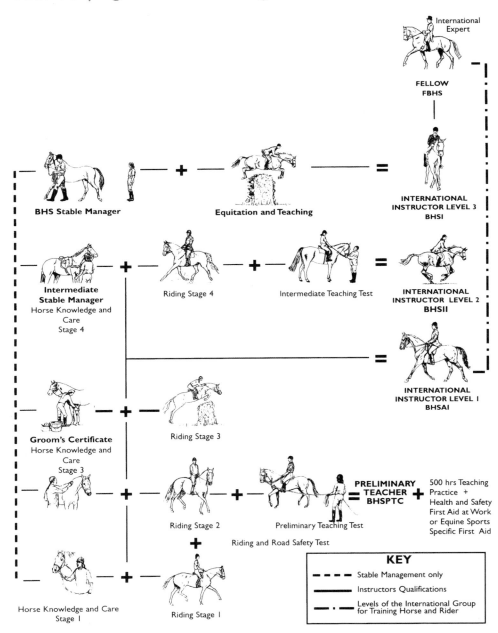

International
Expert

**FELLOW
FBHS**

**INTERNATIONAL
INSTRUCTOR LEVEL 3
BHSI**

BHS Stable Manager

Equitation and Teaching

**Intermediate
Stable Manager**
Horse Knowledge and
Care
Stage 4

Riding Stage 4

Intermediate Teaching Test

**INTERNATIONAL
INSTRUCTOR LEVEL 2
BHSII**

**INTERNATIONAL
INSTRUCTOR LEVEL I
BHSAI**

Groom's Certificate
Horse Knowledge and
Care
Stage 3

Riding Stage 3

Riding Stage 2

Preliminary Teaching Test

**PRELIMINARY
TEACHER
BHSPTC** **+** 500 hrs Teaching
Practice +
Health and Safety
First Aid at Work
or Equine Sports
Specific First Aid

Riding and Road Safety Test

Horse Knowledge and Care
Stage I

Riding Stage I

KEY

- - - - Stable Management only

———— Instructors Qualifications

— · — · Levels of the International Group
for Training Horse and Rider